THE SUPER-SHOPPER'S GUIDE TO NAME-BRAND, DESIGNER AND BARGAIN SHOPPING

OTHER BOOKS IN THE SERIES

SUZY GERSHMAN

BORN TO SHOP
PARIS

THE SUPER-SHOPPER'S GUIDE TO NAME-BRAND, DESIGNER AND BARGAIN SHOPPING

FIFTH EDITION

HarperPerennial
A Division of HarperCollinsPublishers

HarperCollins books may be purchased for educational, business, or sales promotional use. For information, please write: Special Markets Department, HarperCollins Publishers, Inc., 10 East 53rd Street, New York, NY 10022.

FIRST EDITION
Designed by C. Linda Dingler
ISSN 1066-2790
94 95 96 97 ◆/RRD 10 9 8 7 6 5 4 3

Although every effort has been made to ensure the accuracy of prices appearing in this book, please keep in mind that with inflation and a fluctuating rate of exchange, prices will vary. Dollar estimations of prices were made based on the following rate of exchange: 5 French francs = $1 U.S.

To My Mothers:
Gloria Verstein Kalter
Barbara Joseloff Cohen
who live in my heart, and always in Paris

BORN TO SHOP PARIS
Editorial Director: Suzy Gershman
British correspondent: Ian Cook
Paris correspondent: Pascale-Agnes Renaud
Executive Editor: Carol Cohen
Assistant to Executive Editor: Pat Bear
Line Editor: Jill Parsons
Associate Editor: Erica Spaberg
Manager, Publishing Reference Technology: John Day
Computer Production Editor: Douglas Elam

CONTENTS

2 MONEY MATTERS

3 NEIGHBORHOODS

4 REAL-LIFE RESOURCES

8 PARIS TOURS AND DAY TRIPS

PREFACE

Lafayette, I *am here*. Or something like that. Well guys, this is it. You have in your hands my personal guide to Paris—a long time in coming.

You probably know this book as *Born To Shop: France*, but *voilà*, almost ten years later it's here, my own edition—from me to you—a book dedicated almost wholly to Paris. It's chockablock with Paris details, although I did squeeze in a day trip to Brussels (go on a Saturday for the flea markets) and one to Versailles.

This edition is based on the previous ones, so you'll see a lot of familar touchstones. But this updated version has been completely checked to weed out the old (Catherine has closed!), to add many new stores and listings and, more importantly, to put new kinds of consumer information into the pages. In so doing, I have stuck to the original rules:

- The stores visited never knew who I was—all shopping and reporting is always done anonymously.
- No store can buy a listing in this book or any other book in this series.
- I have visited each shop again during the revision period, so each listing in this book has been visited recently, and probably visited twice.
- All opinions expressed are my own—this is a very opinionated book.
- These books are updated and revised regularly, but if you catch a change before I do, please drop a card or a note:

  Born to Shop
  HarperCollins Publishers, Inc.
  10 East 53rd Street
  New York, NY 10022

ACKNOWLEDGMENTS

Paris has changed a lot for me in the last few years: my sister-in-law, who I used to visit in Paris often, died suddenly; my long-time friends from Catherine—the duty free store—went out of business; Pascale-Agnes moved to Belfort; my favorite concierge at the Hôtel Meurice retired (I must be getting old); and even my regular pizza place, around the corner from the "Meurice," went out of business. Of course, I found another one (Pizzeria Venus), but Paris has led me to a series of adjustments.

Happily, old friends have gotten me through the hard times and new friends have come along to teach me new Parisian tricks, so this edition reflects old comforts and new pleasures.

I thank my French family for their help and their love, as well as their translating, their driving, their shopping tips, their hospitality and their lessons on French life style: Marie Jo and Gerard Bizien (as well as Pierre Andre and Marthe Bizien); Pascale-Agnes Renaud—her mother Danielle and her husband Thierry Sahler are part of the soul of this book, and Cathy Nolan, my own American in Paris, who keeps me up to date on all things stylish.

Special thanks to Carolyn Bloodworth, who let me take her to Paris for a few days and taught me gobs of stuff about what first-timers want to see; hugs to Jean-Louis Ginibre.

Kisses on both cheeks to Douglas Elam at HarperCollins, my computer guru, who got this book onto diskette and held my hand while I struggled through a new program. His patience is edited into every page of this book; John Day trained me on the new computer program and never yelled once. Without these guys, the book you have in your hands would never have been possible.

Warm thanks to Dominique Borri, who always provides a wonderful welcome—and often the same room—at the Hôtel Meurice, which has been my shopping headquarters for over a decade now. Jean may have retired, but Victor remains on hand to help me and welcome me back each year. Paris would not be Paris without the "Meurice." Suzanne Gryner at the Paris Intercontinental helped me to expand my horizons and look across the street; thanks to Charles Mardicks, who suggested I try shopping from both Intercontinental hotels. Merci to all.

I must also thank the entire ground staff for American Airlines at Orly Sud and everyone ever associated with American, especially in Paris. I chose American for all my trips simply because they were so fabulous to me after I missed my first plane. I've never missed a flight in my life and when I stood there, almost in tears, they came through calmly and professionally. I got to see the wonderful new terminal in Chicago; I was home almost on schedule. Thanks also to British Airways, my regular fly between London and Paris.

Special thanks to Ian Cook, whom I first met in a fountain in Paris, who took the picture for the cover. I'm eating breakfast at Les Deux Magots and it was even my birthday. And yes, I bought that silly hat at the flea market.

There is a little carousel in the Tuileries right outside my room in the Hôtel Meurice. I ride it every time I come to Paris. As I go round, I remember walking in this park every year since I was seventeen years old; I remember my mother, and the mother I adopted and my sister-in-law, and I grow old and I grow young, and I am in Paris one more time.

INTRODUCTIONS

Well, if you have decided to open this guide and follow Suzy Gershman's path, I have a feeling I like you already. You are in Paris or, if you are not here physically, you are ready for your dreams to transport you here.

You are curious to discover the glories of my city. Let me be the first to tell you that whether you choose a humble shop or a luxury house, someone behind the counter is waiting to tempt you with the charm of Paris! Shopping in Paris is the best way to breathe Paris.

I was born in this city, and am one of the few with four generations of Parisians above me on both my mother and father's side. I like Paris for its vitality, its roots still emerging at the surface, its head in the clouds, its music and its palette of colors, enhanced by the green of its trees.

If you are in town, come to Hermès. If the exit has the potential to be expensive, at least the entrance is free of charge. But, do me a favor before you enter: give a generous look at our windows. The "art of window display" was invented here around 1922 by Emile Hermès. He commissioned the talented Annie Beaumel to make people dream of Hermès when discovering its products through these windows, open to the world. Madame Beaumel remained with Hermès for 52 years. Old Parisians remember that during the German occupation, the inventiveness of the Hermès windows gave them a sparkle of beauty and hope. There were few objects (no leather or silk was available during the war), but a little humor, much harmony, and a lot of color.

Today, the tradition lives on: Leïla Menchari succeeded Madame Beaumel as the fair lady of our window displays. But, I should not talk so much about Hermès in an introduction to shop-

ping all over Paris. You will see for yourself that
each shopkeeper in Paris has his own history,
and a bit of the history of the city inside his
heart. Open your ears, your eyes, not only your
wallets. I conversed with you as a friend and
hope that, through Suzy, you will make many
other friends in Paris.

Bienvenue, welcome!

Jean-Louis Dumas-Hermès
Hermès

Bienvenue and welcome to Paris. I welcome you
to the City of Light as I have welcomed Suzy
Gershman, her family and the other Born to Shop
team members for many years. And I especially
welcome you to a very new edition of this book.
This is the first Born to Shop book devoted entirely
to Paris.

While Suzy Gershman and her family have
been staying in this hotel for many years before
the first edition of this book was even conceived,
we still like to say that Born to Shop was actually
born here. The original partners all stayed here
on their first official reporting job, and their first
encounter with photographer Ian Cook (who took
the cover photograph of this book) took place not
only here at the Meurice, but at our nearby fountain at the Place Concorde.

So you see, we all go back a long way. The
readers of this book have become our extended
family. It is my pleasure now to welcome you as
members of the Born to Shop family, to our hotel:
your home away from home; your shopping
headquarters in Paris.

If you are not a guest here, please come by to
look around and say hello. Have a cup of tea. Put
up your feet, put down your shopping bags. We
look forward to welcoming you in person.

Philippe Roche
General Manager
Hôtel Meurice

Paris

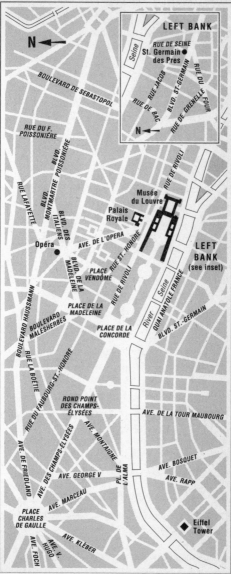

N ←

LEFT BANK

Seine

RUE DE SEINE

St. Germain des Pres ●

RUE JACOB

RUE DE BAC

BLVD. ST-GERMAIN

RUE DU FOUR

RUE DE GRENELLE

N ←

BOULEVARD DE SEBASTOPOL

RUE DU F. POISSONIÈRE

BLVD. MONTMARTRE POISSONIÈRE

RUE DE RIVOLI

RUE LAFAYETTE

BLVD. DES ITALIENS

Musée du Louvre

Palais Royale

Opéra ●

AVE. DE L'OPÉRA

RUE ST-HONORE

BLVD. DE LA MADELEINE

PLACE VENDÔME

RUE DE RIVOLI

LEFT BANK (see inset)

Seine

River

PLACE DE LA MADELEINE

QUAI ANATOLE FRANCE

BOULEVARD MALESHERBES

BOULEVARD HAUSSMANN

PLACE DE LA CONCORDE

BLVD. ST-GERMAIN

RUE LA BOÉTIE

RUE DU FAUBOURG-ST-HONORE

ROND POINT DES CHAMPS-ÉLYSÉES

AVE. DE LA TOUR MAUBOURG

AVE. DE FRIEDLAND

AVE. DES CHAMPS-ÉLYSÉES

AVE. MONTAIGNE

AVE. GEORGE V

PL. DE L'ALMA

AVE. BOSQUET

AVE. RAPP

AVE. MARCEAU

PLACE CHARLES DE GAULLE

AVE. KLÉBER

AVE. V. HUGO

AVE. FOCH

◆ Eiffel Tower

Paris Arrondissements

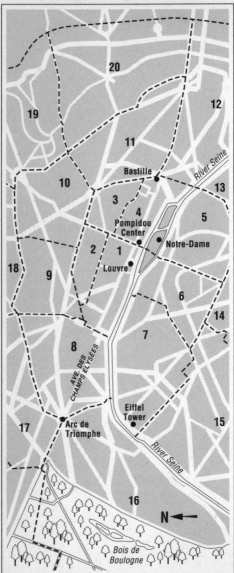

CHAPTER ONE

PARIS DETAILS

Welcome to Paris

Bienvenue and welcome to Paris. It just doesn't get much better than this. Paris is a city of unending beauty, of architecture and flowers and pastries and yes, yes, yes (*mais oui*): shopping.

After your first evening in town you'll know why Paris has been dubbed the City of Light. Sure, you'll see all the glorious lights on all the glorious buildings (even the I.M. Pei pyramid at the Louvre is lit from within), but you're also going to feel light—light-headed from all the shopping opportunities spied throughout the day; all the style yet to come. Whether you are in Paris for a day or a week, you'll be hard-pressed not to go gaga. Paris was invented for fashion; you can't make your way back home without carrying a few shopping bags!

Despite dollar doldrums and international recessions, you need not seriously worry about your pocketbook. You can afford to bring home a few pieces of Paris. Admittedly, Paris isn't a steal, but you can easily trip the light fantastic and come home with more than a few happy memories.

A lot more.

Paris is one of the world's premier shopping cities. Even people who hate to go shopping enjoy it in Paris. What's not to like? The couture-influenced ready-to-wear? The street markets?

The most extravagant kids' shops in the world? Jewelers nestled together in shimmering elegance? Fruits and vegetables piled in bins as if they too were jewels? Perfumes and cosmetics at a fraction of their U.S. cost? Antiques and collectibles that are literally the envy of kings? It's not hard to go wild with glee at your good luck and good sense for having chosen such a place to visit.

Paris Plans

Paris may be one of Europe's biggest capital cities, but it's a simple city to shop—once you know what you're doing. It's all logistics—you can easily combine sightseeing, museum-hopping and *café*-nobbing with almost constant window shopping. While most of the glamorous boutiques are clustered in about four distinct and not-that-far-apart neighborhoods, when you want to get to the real bargains, you need to do a bit of traveling. You'll want to plan each day carefully to fit in all your priorities. (See Chapter Three for more on Paris Neighborhoods.)

Unless you have scads of time on your hands, you'll find shopping in Paris involves making choices: You'll always be sorry you didn't get to one neighborhood or another, but you'll always have an excuse for returning to the City of Light. No matter how little you have time for, you'll still have no trouble spending your budget or finding something worth buying.

A map is called a *plan* in French, so start planning for your savings before you leave home—or as soon as you arrive in your hotel. Pick up one of those free maps of Paris at your hotel and get a feel for the relationship between the sights you want to see, the places where you want to eat and the areas you want to shop. Makes plans with your *plan* in hand.

If you have a map at home, spend a little time doing what I do: make charts that outline each day and your goals for that day. I rarely get everything done (I go much slower than I think I will) but at least my time, my directions, my transportation and my shopping priorities have been thought out and organized to maximize my Paris power.

Bargain Smarts

Prices in Paris are not low, so to sniff out the bargains you're going to need some background information—the bargains go to the shopper who is ready to recognize them, and that means doing some homework.

- If you have favorite designers or targets of acquisition for your trip, shop the major department stores and U.S.-based boutiques for comparison prices. Don't assume you will get a bargain on a Parisian purchase. Many international designer-retailers set prices that are just about the same all over the world.
- If you do not live in a city that has a lot of European merchandise, do some shopping through *Vogue* and *Harper's Bazaar*. In the ads for the designer boutiques, you'll find phone numbers. Call and ask about prices and sales. Don't be afraid to explain that you are contemplating a shopping trip to Europe and are doing some comparison pricing.
- Read French magazines to get familiar with looks, shops, and life styles. They cost a fortune (sometimes $14 a magazine), but many libraries have these magazines; or splurge on a French hairstylist just to read their magazines as you wait.
- Understand the licensing process. Designers sell the rights to their names, and often their

designs, to various makers around the world. Two men's suits may bear an identical label—of a well-known French designer—but will fit differently because they are manufactured differently. Ditto a pair of YSL sunglasses or even a shade of Lancôme makeup. Understand that the styles you see in the U.S. may not even be available in Paris.

- French cosmetics and fragrances can be extraordinarily less expensive in France, or so marginally less that it doesn't pay to schlepp them home. Know prices before you leave home.

- Don't be fooled into thinking that merchandise with foreign-sounding names is made in Europe. Because Americans are so taken by European names, many American-made products have foreign, especially French, names. Since the biggest rage in France these days is American-made products, don't be lured into buying something in France that could be bought at home for less.

The Moscow Rule of Shopping

The Moscow Rule of Shopping is one of my most basic shopping rules, and has nothing to do with shopping in Moscow, so please pay attention. Now: The average shopper, in her pursuit of the ideal bargain, does not buy an item she wants when she first sees it, because she's not convinced that she won't find it elsewhere for less money. She wants to see everything available, then return for the purchase of choice. This is a rather normal thought process. If you live in an Iron Curtain country, however, you know that you must buy something the minute you see it, because if you hesitate—it will be gone. Hence the title of my international law: the Moscow Rule of Shopping.

Naturally you can't compare the selection in Paris to what's on hand in Moscow (Russians would swoon at the airport shopping alone) but the fundamental principle is still applicable.

When you are on a trip, you probably will not have the time to compare prices and then return to a certain shop; you will never be able to backtrack through cities, and even if you could, the item might be gone by the time you got back, anyway. What to do? The same thing they do in Moscow: Buy it when you see it, understanding that you may never see it again. But remember, since you are not shopping in Moscow and you may see the same item again, weigh these questions carefully before you go buy:

1) Is this a touristy type of item that I am bound to find all over town?
2) Is this an item I can't live without, even if I am overpaying?
3) Is this a reputable shop, and can I trust what they tell me about the availability of such items?
4) Is the quality of this particular item so spectacular that it is unlikely it could be matched at this price?

If you have good reason to buy it when you see it, do so.

Caveat: The Moscow Rule of Shopping breaks down if you are an antiques or bric-a-brac shopper, since you never know if you can find another of an old or used item, if you can find it in the same condition, or if the price will be higher or lower. It's very hard to price collectibles, so consider doing a lot of shopping for an item before you buy anything. This is easy in Paris, where there are a zillion markets that sell much the same type of merchandise in the collectibles area. At a certain point you just have to buy what you love and be satisfied that you love it.

Unification and You

Will the so-called unification of Europe affect your shopping habits? Not a lot, but some. Since Europeans themselves can't agree on what unification is going to mean to them and will take the rest of this century to work out the basics of the notion, there is not going to be one big sudden change of plan or new set of rules to learn.

The most dramatic affect on American shoppers is on the tax rate refund. Luxury taxes in France have been steadily dropping for years with the hopes that France can align itself with value added taxes in other EEC countries. As a result, the amount you get back on your *détaxe* refund (see page 49) for perfume is dropping.

You'll also see changes in what's for sale in your basic duty free shops, which happen to dot Paris shopping districts (not just the airports). Many duty free stores, which after 1993 will no longer be able to count on sales to fellow Europeans, are widening their merchandise selection to appeal to Americans and Japanese, who can still save in a big way. EEC residents of course can gleefully enjoy the fact that borders will disappear.

Franc-ly My Dear

Sure you can hark back to those days when one dollar was equal to ten French francs, and you can moan and groan all you want. I call that negative thinking. Instead, remember back when the dollar was equal to four francs, which is where the equation stood for years and years. (If you are not old enough to remember, you'll just have to trust me here.) Now that you've readjusted your thinking, things aren't looking so bad, are they? It's all a matter of perspective!

Yes, the price of a room at the Hôtel Meurice is over $300 these days (and that's the winter, bargain price); a cup of coffee or a Coca-Cola at a hotel is pretty expensive. Room service—I'm talking the basic continental breakfast for two people—at the Paris Intercontinental Hotel costs almost $50!

But you can beat the system. You can save on transportation, meals and more. Combine your luxury hotel room with some down-and-dirty consumer facts and enjoy the best of both worlds:

- Buy Cokes and mineral water at the grocery store and keep them in the minibar. Every chic Frenchwoman in Europe carries a large tote bag with a plastic bottle of mineral water. Avoid drinking Coke—it's expensive everywhere. If you must splurge, enjoy one in your room—after you've bought the six-pack at the market. A whole six-pack costs about the same as one minibar Coke!

- If you take items from the minibar in your room—provided the minibar is not electronically controlled—replace them yourself by shopping at a market for identical items. Make sure you buy the right size packages!

- Buy food from fresh markets (one of Paris' most beautiful natural resources), supermarkets and *traiteurs* who sell ready-cooked gourmet meals—hot or cold. You can eat a fabulous French meal for $5–$10 per person this way. An entire rotisserie chicken, which feeds four, costs no more than $6. Pizza is another good buy.

- Do gift shopping either in duty frees (not the airport kind), flea markets or the *hypermarché;* don't scorn those tacky TTs (Tourist Traps) for great $3 gift items. You can also find small giftables in INNO, PRISUNIC or AUCHAN...or in *métro* stops.

Best Buys of Paris

So, what should you buy in France? This list can vary from season to season, of course, but my favorite categories for savings are:

- Perfumes and Cosmetics: I save at least 50% on the Chanel makeup I use. While French designer mascara comes in a lot of colors you can't get in the U.S., the savings here seems to be only a few dollars, if that. My Sisley wrinkle cream and skin goop is half price in Paris.

  Perfume savings get to the heart-stopping level when you make the commitment to spend 1,200 FF (or whatever it takes for the *détaxe*) and then buy all your gifts and all your sweet-smelling needs at one time so you can get the 40% discount (see page 49). I tend to buy those fragrances which have just been introduced in Paris and are not available yet in the U.S. as gift items because then people get a chance to try something very new.

- Limoges: Blame this one on my friend Carolyn—she got the collecting bug from Princess Diana, no less. Carolyn now buys those little Limoges boxes in the pretty shapes—fruits, vegetables, animals, etc. Each box costs between $75–$100 in Paris, but they cost twice as much in the U.S.

- Hermès: I can't blame this one on Carolyn or even Princess Caroline. On those trips to Paris when I tell myself I will not buy a lot of little things and will stick to one important souvenir, I often find myself at Hermès where prices are definitely lower than in New York. Of course, you must buy enough to qualify for the *détaxe* to make this really practical, but if you feel a splurge coming on, consider that the large-size enamel bangle bracelet costs $268 in Paris without *détaxe*; $209 if you buy two and qualify for *détaxe*, or $350 at the duty free at JFK in New York.

- Candies, Foodstuffs and Chocolates: These make great gifts, especially when wrapped in the distinctive styles of one of Paris' premiere food palaces. I buy Maille's tomato soup-colored "Provençale" mustard in grocery stores (no fancy wrap for me, thanks) and give it to foodies around the world—it's unique and special and I haven't found it in any U.S. specialty stores yet. I also stock up on carmelized almonds in beautiful tin boxes (under $10) or create baskets of a variety of fancy foodstuffs; foods make fabulous gifts and souvenirs in the $2–$10 price range (see page 180).

- Collectibles: It's pretty hard to give advice about the ever-changing collectibles market, but the things that catch my eye have all turned out to be bargains when I compared prices at American flea markets (why didn't I buy more?). I bought an empty postcard album—probably from the turn of the century—at the flea market in Vanves, in perfect condition, for $10. I saw a similar one in a dealers' show in Greenwich, CT for $150. I bought a funky straw hat from the 1950s for $40 and a country-style tablecloth for $5. I thought these were fair prices. My plaster virgin from Lourdes for $2 was a steal (see page 118).

- Italian Designer Goods: This isn't for everyone—but here goes. If you are traveling on to Italy, and you plan to buy expensive designer merchandise, you'll find that prices are high in Italy and you won't get the VAT refund you crave. If you qualify for the French *détaxe* on these same items, they will cost less in Paris than Italy. So buy Gucci in Paris instead of the city of origin.

- French Finds: There are some items you can't

buy any place in the world except France; Paris is as good a place as any to pick them up. Some like to bring home a case of wine. I fall for simpler, easier-to-carry cultural delights: *fèves* and *santons*. A *fève* is a small charm (usually porcelain) that is baked into a special cake that is served from Christmas until Epiphany. The charms have a ranking to them, so that Baby Jesus is the best, a king is good and Goofy doesn't rank too high. (Yes, there are Disney *fèves*.) *Fèves* are, however, collectible. Buy yours in the flea markets (10 francs each; 30 francs for a really good one) or at kitchen supply stores (see page 198). *Santons* are small- to medium- sized carvings of local French country characters; they aren't that easy to find in Paris (try the Place Saint-Sulpice) but if you keep an eye out at flea markets and stores specializing in country wares you will find some.

• Kitsch: I'll admit up front that I adore kitsch. I can't help but buy kitschy souvenirs for myself and my friends. My usual hangout is the Rue de Rivoli (just up the street from the Meurice and the Intercontinental); every day I find another reason to buy a pencil with the Eiffel Tower attached by a slim gold chain, a bath sponge that looks like the French flag, a scarf with tacky illustrations of Paris' best sights, boxer shorts emblazoned with *baguettes* or a T-shirt from the Sorbonne. These items are carefully priced with tourists in mind and never cost more than $10. While the more tasteful part of me wants to advise you not to load up on tacky gifts and instead save your money for something worthwhile, the truth is, I can't stop buying (and using) this junk. It's also fun for kids (or adults) to get creative with: I removed the medallions from a series of cheap key chains and attached them to a necklace—Chanel style—

for a strong fashion statement and a sensational souvenir. Let your imagination take
over when the price is right (see page 100).

Some things are simply not a bargain in any
sense. Unless you are desperate, avoid buying:

- American-made goods—whether from
  designers like Ralph Lauren, Joan & David or
  simply Levi-Strauss, ditto for British goods
  (Aquascutum, Hilditch & Key or Marks &
  Spencer);
- Men's business attire;
- American or English paperbacks or travel
  books;
- Coca-Cola at bars, *cafés* or hotels (see above);
- Postcards priced at $1 or more (you can do
  better, see page 37);
- Massive amounts of EuroDisney souvenirs;
- Big-name designer clothes unless they are
  on sale, you qualify for the *détaxe* or are mar-
  ried to a millionaire.

Information, Please

The French Tourist Office in the U.S. has
installed a new 900 number, which costs 50¢ per
minute; the average call takes five minutes. Everyone who answers the phone speaks English. They
will mail any booklets or brochures you request
(some of them have coupons for discounts), or
will provide you with firsthand information. Dial
900-990-0040. They do not make actual bookings
but will guide you to a local travel agent if you
need one.

If you prefer to go directly to the French
Tourist office, there are several in the U.S.; call
the one nearest you: 212-315-0888 (New York);
312-337-6301 (Chicago); 214-720-4010 (Dallas) or
310-271-6665 (Los Angeles).

The French Government Tourist Office has also

initiated Club France in order to provide information and discounts to American Francophiles.
Membership costs about $75 a year (each addi-
tional family member is $35) but you get a quar-
terly newsletter, upgrade and/or discount
coupons for hotels and car rentals, a Paris
Museum Pass and a few other perks. Write: Club
France, c/o French Government Tourist Office, 610
Fifth Avenue, New York, New York 10020; or call
212-757-0229.

Booking Paris/1

There are a few local guidebooks that may
interest you although they are in French and cost
about $20 each: The first is *Paris Pas Cher* by Fran-
coise and Bernard Delthill, published by Flam-
marion. This guide steers locals to good deals in
every area from hotels to eats to clothes. While
they do list designer and discount resources, the
guide has gone downhill in recent years and
tends toward store promotions. It is in French, is
published annually (date on the cover) and is
available at any bookstore in Paris.

Paris Pas Cher has done so well that there is a
copycat: *Paris Combines*. Although this book has
twice as many listings it's only half as much fun
to read, but is competing because of perceived
value. It comes with a credit card that can be
punched out of the jacket and used in certain
stores for a small discount (usually 5% to 10%).
You need to have a far better grasp of French to
read the second book.

Unless you are spending a lot of time in Paris,
you can probably do just fine without these
guides. All you need is a copy of *Paris Par
Arrondissement*. Several publishers put out this
book, in various sizes and bindings. This is your
source for street maps and bus and *métro* guides.
Mine fits in the palm of my hand and is so com-

plete that I can look up an address in the front of the book then check a chart to find the nearest *métro* stop for that destination.

Booking Paris/2

French magazines are my secret passion—I spend a lot of my time in Paris in my tub, on a park bench or in bed simply strolling through the pages. I can't even read French. Never mind. The ads alone are fabulous; picture pages make universal sense. I like my horoscope (*Bellier*) in French—even though I can only understand about five words. I probably spend $100 at the newsstand on every trip to Paris. If you want to splurge, but not go quite so far, here's my ranking of the best magazines. By the way, I bring mine home to share with friends. They make great gifts and you don't feel like a fool for throwing them away after one read...they do weigh a ton, however.

Vogue: Always my first purchase, partly because of familiarity, partly because this one magazine captures the middle-aged essence of what I want in a fashion magazine. You'll pay about $8 for the privilege.

L'Officiel: Slightly kickier than *Vogue* from a visual standpoint but rather similar—you may find this more interesting if you want something new. Covers high fashion. Another $8 please.

Marie Claire Bis: There's *Marie Claire* in regular editions and then the "bis" which are special editions—I buy both and swear by their home furnishings editions (*Marie Claire Maison*). Young and hip but accessible to real people—not just jet setters. Cost: $6.

Femme: Younger (and cheaper) than those above, it offers a wider range of editorial subjects while still hitting fashion, beauty and lifestyle. About $4.

Elle: The inspiration for the familiar U.S. publishing gem, this modern, perky weekly (it's monthly in the U.S.) statement on fashion and trends should be a staple. About $2.50.

W *Europe*: This is fun for a look-see, if not part of your regular magazine diet—a European edition of W in large-size magazine format. It's in French and covers fashion and design trends all over Europe. Around $6.

Figaro: This fabulous French newspaper offers a huge weekend edition. The Saturday edition has a women's magazine insert ($5.00); the Wednesday edition ($3.00) contains Figaroscope, a weekly agenda of cultural events and travel, sports and restaurants, as well as charts for everything scheduled on the weekend.

Paris Capitale: This slick (and expensive) monthly magazine is sold on newsstands ($3.50). It offers editorials, features and tons of gorgeous pictures, as well as a complete listing of what's happening in town.

Allo Paris is a freebie given away by hotels—it's published weekly and lists basics for museums, cinemas and cultural events.

Sleeping Paris

When it comes to hotels in Paris, I can't stop gathering information. While my home away from home has been the Hôtel Meurice for over a decade, I've also learned to branch out according to hotel promotions and deals (especially deals that are frozen in dollars) and I love to find those cute little hotels with fabulous shopping locations and price tags under $200 a night—which is a bargain for a Paris hotel of the stylish nature. In fact, when you're talking top-of-the-line luxury, a room for under $400 a night is a bargain.

I've developed my own standard for selecting a hotel. I search out several hotels with varying rates that are all in the same neighborhood. I figure that once I know my way around town—once I know where the local grocery store is and have learned the shortcuts from the *métro*—I hate to lose valuable shopping time by learning a new neighborhood. My place in Paris is the 1er; I have a trio of hotels that I frequent (the Meurice, the Intercontinental Paris, the Hôtel Louvre) that are all on the same street and offer the soul of my Paris to me. They are all wonderful hotels offering differing degrees of elegance and price.

If my methods are too linear for you, not to worry. I've found some other treats as well. Remember, if money is an object (isn't it always?) and you don't mind the commute, you can get a hotel room for four at EuroDisney for about $100 a night.

HÔTEL MEURICE

The Meurice is small and quiet, but drop-dead elegant. I think it's fancier than the Ritz and certainly better located—the Rue de Rivoli is out the door, you can walk to shops everywhere, several *métro* stops are nearby and ANGELINA—a tea room of famous proportions—is your mainstay. Breakfast is served in the most beautiful salon in Paris; tea is a must for an after-shopping treat or simply as an excuse to peek into this world of old-fashioned charm. Because the Meurice is a CIGA hotel, you get the benefit of various promotions such as prices that are frozen in dollars. Room rates are seasonal but—get this—August is considered out of season by the French (who flee Paris) so you get more value in August than after September 15, when rates soar until winter sets in. Room rates in promotional deals are for the room, they are not on a per-person basis. They include full breakfast buffet for two, as well as taxes and service. Frequently CIGA promotions let you combine hotels in different parts of Europe at one discounted package price—ask. If you have only one life to live, this is what memories are made of. We've booked for New Year's Eve 1999. (U.S. reservations: 800-221-2340)

HÔTEL MEURICE

228 Rue de Rivoli, 1er (*Métro*: Tuileries or Concorde)

HOTEL INTERCONTINENTAL PARIS

Why would anyone need two hotels located directly across the street from each other? Well, I'll tell you! I get the benefit of my faithful neighborhood and all that is known to me and can still go for special rates at the Intercontinental when they have promotions that are to die for—as they often do. This hotel has a nice old-fashioned feel to it that makes it comfortable without being as fancy as the Meurice. They have a million shops in the hotel and a great newsstand that I rely on no matter which hotel I'm staying at. A recent summer promotion froze rates in dollars and offered a room for $249! This is just too good a deal to pass up. You will not have the same heady feeling of staying at the Meurice, but you will get all the luxury you need and expect while saving a bundle—and that's a pretty good feeling too. This is the hotel for those who want to be practical while still enjoying luxury and service. The Hotel Intercontinental Paris is also a great place if you are travelling with kids and don't want to give up on style but don't want top-of-the-line luxury. (U.S. reservations: 800-327-0200)

Also note that just a few blocks away (although in the 9^e and off my linear theory), Intercontinental has another hotel called Le Grand Hotel Intercontinental. It's got the newly refurbished feeling of a brand new hotel (even though it's in a grand-dame building with a ballroom designed by Garnier!). They take groups and conventions, but it has a fabulous location for shoppers (one block from GALERIES LAFAYETTE) and for those who want to take in EuroDisney, the

RER train station to Marne La Vallée is across the street. The rooms are teeny tiny but you can get the same promotional rates during special sales. (U.S. reservations: 800-327-0200)

HOTEL INTERCONTINENTAL PARIS
  2 Rue du Castiglione, 1er (Métro: Concorde)

LE GRAND HOTEL INTERCONTINENTAL
  2 Rue Scribe, 9e (Métro: Opéra)

HÔTEL DU LOUVRE

This is a small old-fashioned hotel that's a member of the Concorde group. This means you have the owners of the Crillon (one of Paris' fanciest hotels) as your landlord and the benefit of a fabulous discount program used throughout the Concorde chain. While you can't get a room at the Crillon for less than $200, you can get one at the Hôtel du Louvre—and many other Concorde hotels—for about $175. You can get various special rate packages; you can get prices frozen in dollars! Not every hotel in the chain is my kind of place (some are great, some are so-so) but the Hôtel du Louvre is a winner. The hotel overlooks Opéra and is situated directly across the street from the Louvre. Its modern rooms are decorated with Laura Ashley, French style. My favorite room has a gabled roof, blue and white tile everywhere and a gigantic bathroom with glass doors that overlook Opéra. Tour groups have discovered this hotel (its only drawback) but the location, the price and the charm more than make up for the bother. (U.S. reservations: 800-888-4747)

HÔTEL DU LOUVRE
  Place Andre Malraux, 1er (Métro: Palais-Royal)

Small Finds

If you prefer small neighborhood hotels to members of chains or big groups, try some of these local hang-outs. Contact them directly to make your best deal.

HOTEL BALZAC

An old hotel that has been modernized to combine a deluxe visit to Paris with an intimate atmosphere. Some rooms are complete with a stunning view of the Eiffel Tower. Located at the top of the Étoile, right off the Champs-Élysées. The Rue Balzac is a teeny-tiny street; this is a teeny hotel with only seventy charming rooms. A real find. (Telephone: 45-63-84-28)

HOTEL BALZAC
6 Rue Balzac, 8ᵉ (Métro: George V)

HOTEL SAINTS-PÈRES

This small hotel has the tiniest rooms in France, but a great location on the Left Bank and an excellent price. Fashion buyers stay here, as do fashion editors. The most famous room in the house, number 100, has a fresco on the ceiling, and is worth booking ahead for, if you like a rococo giggle. Otherwise the rooms are modern and sparse; but the lobby is a breath of spring, with its glass-enclosed patio and small bamboo bar. (Telephone: 45-44-50-00)

HOTEL SAINTS-PÈRES
65 Rue des Saints-Pères, 6ᵉ (Métro: Sèvres-Babylone)

MAYFAIR HOTEL

The best-kept secret in Paris, the Mayfair is one block from the Meurice. There's no doorman, no hoopla. You could pass by without ever knowing what's within. The Mayfair is small, intimate, and family-run, with a very well-dressed and knowing clientele. The rooms are done in the Regency style; there's a hair dryer in the bathroom. One block from Concorde, a few steps off the Rue de Rivoli, this hotel just might offer the best deal in Paris if you can't get one of Intercontinental's special deals. (Telephone: 42-60-38-14)

MAYFAIR HOTEL
3 Rue Rouget de Lisle, 1ᵉʳ (*Métro*: Concorde)

HOTEL DE SEINE
Since the Rue de Buci is one of my favorite streets in Paris, there's every reason why I would love this small hotel nestled into the heart of the left bank and half a block from the Rue de Buci. They don't take credit cards, but a double room was 800 francs when I last poked in, so just have extra traveler's checks on hand. The feel is country French but there's color TV and everything you need. Even a hair dryer. Left Bank hotels are always teeny tiny so don't expect Texas proportions. (Telephone: 46-34-22-80)

HOTEL DE SEINE
52 Rue de Seine, 6ᵉ (*Métro*: Saint-Germaine-des-Prés)

HOTEL DU JEU DE PAUME
My friend Joel from *People* magazine found this one and it's on the Ile de Saint Louis to boot. Room with a bath was 730 francs for one or two people; for 820 francs you got a garden as well! Some rooms have timbered ceilings but the decor can be annoyingly modern and sterile. This isn't my choice, but Joel feels strongly that you should have the option. With only 32 rooms and a few apartments and suites, book early. A full apartment for four costs about $400 a night. (Telephone: 40-46-02-76)

HOTEL DU JEU DE PAUME
54 Rue Saint Louis en l'Ile (*Métro*: Pont-Marie)

HOTEL MONTAIGNE
Located on the toniest shopping street in all of Paris, this hotel is directly across from the five-star Plaza Athénée, yet offers elegance on a smaller scale. The rooms feel like a friendly Hilton but since they are about $200 a night, you cannot complain. Everything is new and modern—only 29 rooms. (Telephone 47-20-30-50)

Hotel Montaigne
  6 Avenue Montaigne, 8e (*Métro*: Alma Marceau)

Flying to Paris

From the U.S.: While getting to Paris may seem easy enough—after all, most major carriers fly there—I've got a few secrets that might make getting there more fun...and less expensive.

- Not only are winter airfares always the best prices, but they are often accompanied by promotional ticketing gimmicks. For instance: You pay for one ticket and get the second ticket at half price...no matter what class service you book, or you can bring a companion for a discounted price, or you can bring the kids. In fact, Sabena just ran a summer promotion that allowed you to bring kids for free! There are deals out there.
- During winter, frequent flyer miles may go on sale via your favorite airline. Imagine my surprise to learn that American Airlines and Delta both had winter deals whereby a business class ticket to Paris cost a mere 60,000 miles (economy = 40,000!). These are unadvertised specials, so call around and ask! (For comparison's sake, 60,000 miles was the regular amount for a coach ticket on American, and Delta just raised their price for coach to 70,000 miles.) Off season is the way to go.
- Try ticket brokers and travel clubs for deals. I often call Moment's Notice (Hot line: 212-750-9111), which is a firm specializing in selling trips that no one else has bought—at discounted prices. Moment's Notice, which normally requires a membership fee, will let you join up after you've found a deal you want. Don't expect to get mileage points on one of these deals. Sometimes I call just to listen to their tape.

- Check out consolidators who will unload unsold tickets on scheduled flights for discount prices (which vary with the season, as do regular prices). Again, no frequent flyer miles. These tickets are great for last minute travelers who may not qualify for 21-day advance purchase prices. You need only about four business days notice. I called Unitravel (800-325-2222) and was offered roundtrip New York to Paris for $628 plus departure tax on Northwest Airlines during summer peak. You pay by credit card on the phone; they Fed Ex the tickets to you at no extra charge. C.L. Thomson is another consolidator, but they must be contacted by travel agent (800-833-4258).

- Packages that include airfare and hotel always give you good prices, especially if you can get those prices guaranteed in dollars, which is possible through many big wholesalers, airlines and hotels. If the dollar is depressingly low, or merely unstable enough to make you nervous, look carefully at deals in which prices are frozen in U.S. dollars. Car rental agencies also have some of these offerings. Don't forget to check out EuroDisney packages that include airfare, hotel and transfers. You can easily bop into Paris on a day-to-day basis.

- Air France doesn't advertise this, but if you book a trip to Paris through Jet Vacations (800-JET-0999), you will get a charter price on a regularly scheduled Air France flight! You could call Air France and book the exact same ticket and pay more for it (if you really wanted to do something so stupid). Repeat: Although Jet Vacations offers charter rates, they are not operating no-name charter planes. You will fly on regularly scheduled Air France flights. But there are a limited number of seats, so be advised. In-flight movies and stereo are complimentary, there's duty free shopping on the plane and the seats are guaranteed. This may not be the least expensive way to get to Paris, but it is one of the best, and it is far less expensive than regular rates on Air France.

- British Air doesn't advertise this as much as they should, but they too have a deal. Not a charter flight, but a choice of a number of packages that include London and Paris and happen to be the single best way to get both cities into one trip for a price. Call (800) 247-9297.

- Call Now Voyager to volunteer to be a free-lance courier; you'll get a roundtrip ticket for about $200, although your luggage allowance is severely restricted. That means you get to take only one carry-on measuring about 9×14×22 inches and a freight company may have your baggage allowance. Most flights are international and leave from New York or Newark; some departures are from Miami and Houston. Trips usually last one week; there are some two-week and a few open-ended tickets. Bookings are for singles; if you are with another person, be prepared for your partner to go the day before or the day after you. Bookings can be made up to two months in advance; they are non-refundable. You pay a $50 registration fee; they take cash or credit cards. Cash offers you a discount. Call (212) 431-1616.

- Air France is part owner of an airline called Air Inter, which is your basic domestic carrier throughout France. For those who are not French residents, there is a France Pass. You cannot buy this ticket in France, so stay awake: The ticket costs a flat fee (about $250), it is valid for one month, and it allows unlimited travel to any of thirty French cities for any seven days during that month.

- Check out new American gateway cities for possible deals. American Airlines is going gung-ho on European expansion. If a new gateway city is opened, promotional prices to introduce the route may be so low that you can't afford to stay home. American has fabulous international service from their Chicago hub. Also note: USAir flies from Philadelphia; Delta has nonstop Orlando to Paris service. There are often promotional rates when these new regional routes open up or plain old special deals to fill seats—check it out!

- I've never flown Tower Air, but they offer deals that cannot be ignored: this charter airline was advertising business class seats to Paris at $349 each way. That means roundtrip of $698 plus taxes (about $25) on their regularly scheduled 747 flights; nonstop every weekend. They also have coach rates. Call 800-34-TOWER.

From the U.K.: Americans, if you think you'll just make a quick little hop from London to Paris on a whim, you may be shocked to realize that the regular airfare between the two cities is outrageously high. British Airways has a special advance booking fare of $200 (roundtrip) which requires a Saturday night stay and is the deal of the century. Call British Air first to coordinate your travel as they may have other deals that make it worthwhile to add in a London layover or visit. To get a deal takes a lot of planning; you might want to call your favorite bucket shop. (That's a travel discounter—for you Yanks.) British Airways has about 75 flights a day to Paris from London and more from other British cities (like Manchester), but better yet are some of their packages which include the airfare, transfers and hotel. British Airways also has several EuroDisney packages that may offer you the best deal. For discounted fares from London, you'll need a bucket shop or an airfare war. If you are already in Paris and want to get to London, check with your hotel concierge for a travel agent.

If you prefer to use the easier Orly airport, or want to fly London–Lille (or elsewhere), note that British Airways has recently taken a share in TAT, a French airline, and can now serve several new French airports. Check out promotional rates and deals.

From Brussels: Don't look at me like that! This is great information. Brussels happens to be just over two hours away from Paris (see page 228) via train; you can easily fly into Brussels and out of Paris (or vice versa) or even go to Paris for the weekend from Belgium. You can also connect on a flight from Brussels to Paris. When there are airfare wars and low-priced tickets to Europe that everyone gobbles up, remember this trick as a way to get to Paris that no one else has thought about. Please note that Air France and Sabena have gone into partnership to offer a strong Brussels hub; you can also use Brussels as a departure to the Orient. Brussels is my travel tip of the moment.

Sabena runs an awful lot of smart promotions. They've had a kids-fly-free deal; they've had glorious winter and weekend rates; they know what they are doing. Also remember that American Airlines flies to both Paris and Brussels, so you can book into one city and out of the other at no extra cost. Do the same thing with British Airways through London.

Training to Paris

The Chunnel (Tunnel under the Channel) connects Britain and France. You can connect to Paris easily from the U.K. by various train routes (to Chunnel or not to Chunnel?) or train-plus-ferry routes; you can arrive in Paris from Brussels in less than two and a half hours. Major train stations are being renovated as we speak and will soon have duty free facilities to ease your international commute. The London–Paris commute, especially for EEC passport holders, will be a breeze.

Arriving in Paris

If you arrive at Orly you'll be welcomed by a small, efficient airport (with 18 duty free shops—so don't worry) and a down-home feel. It's only when you depart that you will panic as you realize there is Orly Nord and Orly Sud, and your ticket probably does not say which you want. Fear not, if you are flying American or Delta, you want Orly Sud.

Orly airport is to the south of Paris and is not as far away from town as CDG (the abbreviation for Charles de Gaulle International Airport), but it's not that close either. Expect a taxi to the 1er to cost you about $35–$40 (including tip).

All major car rental agencies have offices in the airport or you can take either a bus or train into town. Orlyval trains get you to town in 20 minutes; Orlybus takes you directly to the RER station at Denfert-Rochereau (on the edge of Paris) where you can get a taxi or connect to the *métro*. For English language information on Orly transport call 49-75-15-15.

Charles de Gaulle airport is composed of two parts, Terminal 1 and 2. Terminal 1 has various satellites, Terminal 2 has pods designated A–D. A taxi to the 1er from CDG will cost at least $60 if not more. Do note that most French taxis are small; if you have a lot of luggage, hold out for a Mercedes taxi. If you have a lot of family plus a lot of luggage, expect to need two taxis. Or you can send one person and all the luggage in a taxi and let the other members of the family take public transportation. Air France offers bus service from Étoile (take taxi from there); you can take Roissy Rail which lets you off at either the Gare du Nord or Châtelet—a more in-town location. There are two lines of bus service, aside from Air France: one drops you at Nation, the other, at Gare de l'Est. For English language information about transport at CDG, call 48-62-22-80.

If coming from the U.K., coordinate your airports. New TAT flights allow British Airways to use both Paris airports. If you are in and out of London and then on to the U.S., make sure you have the right airport for the transfer.

Getting Around Paris

Paris is laid out in a system of zones called *arrondissements*, which circle around from inside to outside. When France adopted the Zip Code method for its mail, Parisians incorporated the *arrondissement* number into the Zip Code as the last two digits. Thus a Zip Code of 75016 means the address is in the 16th *arrondissement* (16^e). You'll find the *arrondissement* information valuable in planning your shopping expeditions. Check the map frequently, however, since you may think that 1er and 16e are far apart, when in actuality you can walk the distance and have a great time doing so. (Take the Rue du faubourg-Saint-Honoré toward the Champs-Élysées and you even get a tour of the 8e thrown in.)

Note that if you see a number with a small *e* written after it, this number signifies the *arrondissement*. The first *arrondissement*, however, is written 1er. Knowing the proper *arrondissement* is essential to getting around rapidly in Paris. It is also a shorthand system for many people to sum up everything a place can or may become—simply by where it is located or how far it is from something that is acceptably chic.

With its wonderful transportation system, Paris is a pretty easy city to navigate. Tourists are usually urged to ride the *métro*, but buses are available and often a treat—you can see where you're going and get a free tour along the way. Your edition of *Paris Par Arrondissement* usually has bus routes as well as a *métro* map. *Métro* maps are handed out free at your hotel and are printed in zillions of guidebooks. Keep one in your wallet at all times.

You can rent a car in Paris and may want to do so to get out to EuroDisney or the countryside; avoid driving around the Place de la Concorde and you'll be fine. Most car rental agencies will pick up your rental return at your hotel, saving you the time and trouble of returning the car. We returned a car at the Intercontinental on a Sunday, worried that it wouldn't be picked up until Monday and we would be charged for an extra day. Many phone calls later we found that the clock stopped ticking the minute the concierge notified the agency (Hertz) that we were ready!

If you intend to drive around Paris (silly you) be sure you know about the parking regulations and how to work the little meters, which provide a ticket for you to insert in your windshield to prove to the police that you have paid for your curbside parking. Just because you don't see a meter like we have in the U.S. doesn't mean that the parking is free.

Stick to public transportation and any of many *métro* ticket plans for easiest access to the city. If you can speak a little bit of French and visit Paris often enough to take the time to do this, buy a *carte orange*. It is exactly what it sounds like: an orange card, which bears a passport-type photo of yourself. (Bring a photo with you, or use the photo booth in the Concorde station.) The *carte orange* is good for unlimited travel on bus or *métro*.

Once you have your permanent orange card, with your photo in place, you will then only have to buy a *coupon jaune* for each week that you want to travel—I've had the same orange card for about ten years. A weekly *coupon jaune* costs about $10; you may also buy a monthly version (about $40). The *carte orange* is about half the price of the weekly ticket pushed for tourists—bargain shopping begins at the station, folks.

Note: You probably cannot get the *carte orange* unless you speak enough French to negotiate the purchase and can answer a few questions that will be asked; touristy-type tourists will be guided toward other kinds of more expensive ticket arrangements.

- The *carnet* is made up of ten tickets, can be bought at any station, and can be used for the bus or the *métro*. An individual ticket to the *métro* costs about $1 a ride; with the *carnet* the price drops to about sixty cents a journey. Note that Paris has switched from a yellow ticket to a turquoise ticket; if you have old tickets from a trip many years ago they will probably still work. If the electronic gate rejects your ticket, exchange it at the ticket booth.

- *Paris Visite* is a transportation pass providing travel for three to five days (depending on what you buy); it costs up to $30 but includes airport trips, the suburbs and even Versailles, and is really an awfully good deal. The pass comes in a black case in which you insert something that looks remarkably like a *coupon jaune*. This pass is sold at RATP stations (big *métro* stations or RER stations—I look at the acronym and think "rapid transit"), SNCF stations (French national trains) and ADP (airports de Paris) booths—at either airport, Orly or CDG.

- There are Travelcard passes, good for unlimited one-day travel that cost about $5, but remember, the *carte orange* costs about $10, and it's good for a whole week. However, you can't go to Versailles on the *carte orange*, but it only costs about $5 (round trip) for a regular old RER ticket to Versailles anyway. Juggle wisely.

Also please note that the *métro* is continuing to grow—this is not a dead transportation system developed a hundred years ago and left to suffer through the indignities of modern times. New lines and spurs are added; new connections to both RER (local commuter trains) and even TGV (bullet trains outside of Paris) are being added. Watch this space.

Cars in Paris

I cannot imagine that you really want to rent a car in Paris, unless you plan to head for the hills (of Provence, of course). All major car rental agencies are on hand, at airports and all over town. The catch is, if you book your car from the U.S. and participate in a promotional deal, you will get a far better rate and it will be guaranteed in dollars. In fact, free unlimited mileage was recently offered with a rate of $161 a week when Avis advertised their Discover Europe promotion. We realized what a great bargain this was when we rented a car at CDG airport for a few days at EuroDisney and returned the car in Paris ($3 drop-off charge); we paid almost that same rate per day. OK, it was a bigger car and it was red...but really.

Europcar has a program called European Passport that allows you to pick up your car in one city and leave it in another without a serious drop-off charge.

All the major companies have toll-free numbers for European reservations:

Avis: 800-331-1084

Hertz: 800-654-3131

National (Europcar): 800-477-6285

If you want a car and driver, try Carey France at 42-65-54-20, or call their American headquarters: 800-336-4646. You can have a limo, a sedan or even a van—to hold all your packages and shopping bags!

Shopping Hours

Hours in Paris reflect the big city nature of the town, so if you are used to provincial hours (where everything closes for lunch and Monday mornings are shopping poison) you'll be thrilled to know that the pulse of Paris never stops— some stores (most often bookstores and drugstores) are even open late, sometimes as late as midnight.

Mondays can be a tad moody, but generally speaking, *stores are open Monday, or part of Monday*. This is a sharp departure from policy in Italy or even in other parts of France. Those stores that tend toward the Monday morning close (they will open at 3 P.M.) are small stores, Mom and Pop stores or little groceries that were open on Sunday. There happens to be a very strong neighborhood rotation of stores so that every part of town has a few stores open on Sunday—these are usually little markets that function as general stores and provide necessities and foodstuffs. But stores that perform on Sunday often take Monday morning off. Always ask the concierge, or call the shop on a Monday if you want verification.

Summer hours may differ from winter hours (longer openings in the evening; Saturday closings at midday), and many stores in Paris close for lunch on Saturday during the summer.

Outside of Paris, most stores close every day for two hours for lunch. Versailles stays open because of the huge tourist business.

The entire month of August may be unusual.

Most of France closes down on August 15 for the Feast of the Assumption. Bastille Day, July 14, also is a big closing day—although many Parisian retailers try to take advantage of the crowds in the streets and open shop for extra business. (Likewise, some stores will be open in Paris on August 15, but none will be open in the countryside.) Drugstores and *charcuteries* are open on big holidays, but big stores certainly are not. While the old rumor that Paris is dead in August has been laid to rest, some stores do close for two weeks of vacation in August without even sending a postcard to advise you.

Most stores in Paris open between 9:30 A.M. and 10 A.M.—the big department stores tend to open before 10 A.M. while regular retail uses 10 A.M. as the barometer. Stores remain open until 7 P.M. or 7:30 P.M. They may additional hours during the Christmas season. Stores usually are open on saints' days but closed on national holidays.

Shopping Services

Shopping in Paris is either extremely simple because you limit yourself to the very obvious areas, or very complicated because you *know* how much is out there, and that you couldn't possibly conquer it even if all Paris were divided into three parts and you had a month to shop each of them.

Where there's confusion, there's a business. Wives of Americans businessmen in Paris, who cannot get green cards to work in France and are at the mercy of their own imaginations and connections to find employment, very often set up shopping services. If you use this book properly, you should not need a shopping service. However, you should know that they exist.

Ask your concierge to recommend a service and specify if you want an American or not. Expect to pay an hourly rate with a minimum. Car and driver are extra. Or ask the hotel to hire a babysitter for you for a morning or a day. This usually costs $10 an hour. Ask for a young, hip, attractive babysitter who speaks English. When the babysitter comes, ask her to take you shopping.

Maribeth Piccour de Bourgies is an American married to a Frenchman who runs a service offering either tours or an hourly rate. She'll take you (and three friends) to the flea markets in a chauffeured car for about $500. Walking tours are about $50 per person, a day of designer fashion shows costs about $600. Contact Maribeth's firm, Chic Promenade at 43-48-85-04 or fax her at 43-56-64-82.

Sunday in the Park with Georges

Although traditional Parisian retail is closed tight on Sundays, there is still an enormous amount of shopping going on. When someone wishes you a "Bonne Dimanche" he must indeed mean good luck in the street markets, the flea markets, good luck with the goods sold on the quais, from the street vendors in the Beaubourg, from the touristy stores and postcard kiosks and even the museum stores. A bonne dimanche in Paris is when the sky is bright blue, the air is not too hot, the tourists are still asleep, and you and yours are on the prowl—taking in the people of Paris and the things they sell on Sundays.

While LE DRUGSTORE PUBLIS is open on Sundays—and there are many drugstore-type places in Paris, local stores open for this and that—the glory of Sunday shopping is in a fabulous stroll along the banks of the river, the slow and careful wandering through the fruits and vegetable markets and then the flea market, in the crêpe bought from a stand, the people and their dogs who walk in the park and in the hot chocolate you have at ANGELINA when you celebrate the triumphs of the day. For best Sunday shopping try:

- The Flea Market at Vanves (see page 117) and the fruit, vegetable and dry goods market one street over—arrive early, 9 A.M. is just fine, and finish up in time for lunch or even a picnic supplied by the street market;

- Stroll along either side of the river (or both!) where the booksellers and their stalls are most dense—I like to take the *métro* to Hôtel de Ville on the right bank, hop out and cross over to the river bank and stroll the quai here, walking all the way (not that far) to the Village Saint Paul where there are numerous antiques shops. This is a good after-lunch or midday project. The booksellers vary one from the next, some sell antique books, others sell just postcards or prints. Some of these dealers just come to town for the weekends when they open up the little stall, stand by and chat with passersby and then return to other cities and other jobs for the week.

- As mentioned, the Village Saint Paul is open on Sunday afternoons—this is a jumble of antiques shops at street level and a building with some dealers within—all bunched together near Bastille, but at the edge of the river. It's very French, it's very un-touristy and it's in an easy-to-get-to location, especially if you are already out walking on the quai. If you want to *métro* up and then walk elsewhere, get off at Saint Paul and walk toward the river, behind the church (named Saint Paul, of course).

Antiquing on Sundays is very much the national hobby; don't forget to check the newspapers or with your concierge for special shows or events which might be in town for the weekend. From February through April, the weekends are

dense with special events—many of which highlight shows for antiques and/or *brocante* (used
items, not necessarily antique).

When the weather is good, shops in the main
flow of tourist traffic may open on a Sunday just
to catch the extra business. Every now and then a
duty free will open up; TT's near popular attrac-
tions are almost always open on Sunday afternoons. By 5 P.M. on a Sunday, it is hard to find
any place that's open. Except LE DRUGSTORE
PUBLIS.

Snack and Shop

It's hard to get a really bad meal in Paris; the
trick is to find a good meal that's not too expensive. You can count on me to have a nosh at
every *crêpe* stand I pass; I've been to McDonald's
and am not ashamed to tell. I haunt LE DRUG-
STORE PUBLIS on the Left Bank right on Boulevard Saint-Germain across from the famous
church Saint-Germain-des-Prés and I stand by
that old tourist standby, CAFÉ DEUX MAGOTS
(across the street and next to the Church)
because while it may cost $13 for coffee and
croissants for two for breakfast, it beats the $50 for
the exact same breakfast at a fancy hotel. And
there is nothing better than the early morning
air (and light), a French newspaper and a seat at
one of the world's greatest theaters.

I eat a lot of pizza; pizza places are easy to
find in every neighborhood. Or try other fast
foods, like sandwiches or *crêpes* at places like
PIZZA EXPRESS, 10 Rue Cambon or 259 Rue
Saint Honoré, both branches are in the 1er. They
open at 7:30 A.M., so you can get a fresh *croissant*
or low-cost breakfast as well. I eat a lot of *pic-
niques* bought from grocery stores I pass as I wander; you can buy in the street or the grocery
stores of the Rue de Buci any day of the week.

For meals in specific shopping neighborhoods, I depend on:

LA CHOPE DES VOSGES

Located right on the Place des Vosges—in the heart of the Marais—where you certainly will want to spend some of your time anyway, this charming restaurant offers you the choice of lunch, dinner or simply tea, which is served from 3 P.M. to 7 P.M. With its old-fashioned front, stone interior, and wood beams, the multilevel space has all the atmosphere you want from a neighborhood like this. Prices are low to moderate; there is a fixed-price, full meal for about $22. You don't really need reservations for lunch but the telephone number is: 42-72-64-04.

LA CHOPE DES VOSGES

22 Place des Vosges, 3e (Métro: Saint Paul)

LA COUR SAINT-GERMAIN

Be still my heart that flutters to the tune of Pierre Deux fabric! This is that adorable French restaurant you planned to enjoy, but wait! It's not expensive! This is a chain, they serve a fixed-price meal—I consider it French fun for the common man. But it suits me just fine. There is one location near the Champs-Élysées, another right on Boulevard Saint-Germain, smack dab in the middle of the Left Bank's most popular area. The two restaurants offer identical meals and the same ambience, although the Left Bank one is a bit more touristy and crowded. In either restaurant you will have a delicious dinner for about $15 or $20 per person. You can choose from about eight different menus. Dessert is extra.

LA COUR SAINT-GERMAIN

156 Boulevard Saint-Germain, 6e (Reservations: 43-26-85-49) (Métro: Saint-Germain-des-Prés)

18 Rue Marbeuf, 8e (Reservations: 47-23-84-25) (Métro: Franklin D. Roosevelt)

ANGELINA

If you've ever heard of Rumpelmayer's, the famed New York ice cream parlor, then you are beginning to understand Angelina—a Parisian tearoom opened by Rene Rumpelmayer in 1903. Famous for their hot chocolate, the restaurant also happens to be a great place for breakfast, lunch or dinner—salads and easy snacks are a breeze; pastries and desserts are simply the house specialty. You'll see many French people here—especially matrons and daughters; Don't write this off as a touristy joint: it's a grand place to stare at people and feel very French. You'll get so hooked on the place (it's my personal hangout in Paris) that you'll soon want the dishes—and you can have them: a tea set costs about $100. They open for breakfast at 9:30 A.M. and are located beneath the Hôtel Meurice—convenient to all shopping in the 1er, the tourist shops on the Rue de Rivoli and even the Louvre itself. If you're not early or it's a special occasion, make a reservation: 42-96-35-60.

ANGELINA

228 Rue Rivoli, 1er (*Métro:* Concorde or Tuileries)

CAFÉ DE LA PAIX

This is hardly an original thought and is a major tourist haunt. It is said that if you sit at a table in the Café de la Paix you will see everyone you know walk by. Eating here is nonetheless a treat and a part of the Paris fantasy—you're a block from the big department stores and have sufficiently escaped the zoo-like nature of the Blvd. Haussmann. The menu is huge (English and French) so you can pick and chose and find affordable eats; desserts are more expensive than real food. You can use the bathrooms in Le Grand Intercontinental and peek into the Garnier ballroom. You can pretend you knew Hemingway.

This is Opéra as you must enjoy it, at least once. If you are in a big hurry or alone and unhappy about it, eat at the bar.

CAFÉ DE LA PAIX

Le Grand Hotel, 12 Blvd. Capucines, 9e (*Métro*: Opéra)

Postcards from the Edge

Postcards in Paris are as original and arty as the city itelf—there are truly thousands of designs and styles to choose from, but watch out, many of them cost between $1–$2 each! The enormously cute, large-sized Disney cards (sold in Paris, not EuroDisney) cost even more! If you want to save on postcards, stop by the fancy hotels and ask the concierge if he's got postcards—you'll usually get at least one. It pays to be well-dressed for this exercise.

The better the postcard design, the higher the price. Art cards are almost always over $1 each. You can get cards for a mere one franc each if you shop the TT's carefully; you may even luck out and find fifteen cards for ten francs! This takes some doing; anyone who gets a decent card for a franc should be proud of her shopping skills. Walk along the Rue de Rivoli, where the TT's are thick; check prices as you go. The higher uptown you go (away from Concorde, toward Louvre), the less the price. TT's near Notre Dame also have cards for one franc and often offer bulk deals.

Buy stamps at a PTT (post office), a tobacco store or from your hotel concierge. Note that postage to the U.S. (even for a postcard) is rather pricey, but if you have friends in other EEC countries, you'll find postage fairly priced. I buy the cards in Paris but mail them when I get home— only friends in England get theirs from Paris.

Airport Shopping and Duty Frees

Both Orly and CDG have more than their share of shopping opportunities for visitors—in fact, the shopping is so brisk in these airports that they have their own shopping bag. Stores at CDG are fancier than those at Orly, but you will have no trouble dropping a few, or a few hundred, francs. Please note that prices at duty free shops may be slightly cheaper than regular retail in town, but not much. You should have already purchased your cosmetic and fragrance bargains in Paris at the kind of duty free shops that offer 20–40% savings; you will save only 13% at the airport.

The selection at the airport may be better than the selection on your airplane, but airline prices can be better. It pays to bring the duty free price list from your plane and save it for final comparisons if you need to shop at airports.

U.S. Customs and Duties

To make your reentry into the United States as smooth as possible, follow these tips:

- Know the rules and stick to them!
- Don't try to smuggle anything.
- Be polite and cooperative (up until the point when they ask you to strip, anyway...).

Remember:

- You are currently allowed to bring in $400 worth of merchandise per person, duty-free. Before you leave the United States, verify this amount with one of the U.S. Customs offices, as it is expected to change to $1,000. If you miss reading about the change in the newspaper, you may be cheating yourself out of a good deal. Each member of the family is entitled to the deduction; this includes infants.

- Currently, you pay a flat 10% duty on the next $1,000 worth of merchandise. This is extremely simple and is worth doing. I'm saying that under present laws, you may bring in $1,400 worth of goods by paying $100 in duty and this is a small price to make life easy— and crime-free.

- Duties thereafter are based on the type of product. They vary tremendously per item.

- The head of the family can make a joint declaration for all family members. The "head of the family" need not be male. Whoever is the head of the family, however, should take the responsibility for answering any questions the Customs officers may ask. Answer questions honestly, firmly and politely. Have receipts ready, and make sure they match the information on the landing card. Don't be forced into a story that won't wash under questioning. If you tell a little lie, you'll be labeled as a fibber and they'll tear your luggage apart.

- You count into your $400 per person everything you obtain while abroad—this includes toothpaste (if you bring the unfinished tube back with you), gifts, items bought in duty-free shops, gifts for others, the items that other people asked you to bring home for them and—get this—even alterations. Books do not count as part of the $400; they are duty free.

- Have the Customs registration slips for your personally-owned goods in your wallet or easily available. If you wear a Cartier watch, for example, whether it was bought in the United States or in Europe ten years ago, should you be questioned about it, produce the registration slip. If you cannot prove that you took a foreign-made item out of the United States with you, you may be forced to pay duty on it! If you own such items but have no registration or sales slips, take photos or Polaroids of the goods and have them notarized in the U.S. before you depart. The notary seal and date will prove you had the goods in the U.S. before you left the country.

• The unsolicited gifts you mailed from abroad do not count in the $400-per-person rate. If the value of the gift is more than $50, you pay duty when the package comes into the country. Remember, it's only one unsolicited gift per person, and you cannot mail them to yourself.

• Do not attempt to bring in any illegal food items—dairy products, meats, fruits or vegetables (coffee is OK). Generally speaking, if it's alive, it's *verboten*. Any yummy, creamy French cheese is illegal, but a hard or cured cheese is legal.

• Antiques must be a hundred years old to be duty free. If they are one hundred years old they may need permission from the French government to leave the country. Provenance papers will help (so will permission to export the antiquity, since it could be an item of national cultural significance). Any bona fide work of art is duty free whether it was painted fifty years ago or just yesterday; the artist need not be famous.

• Dress for success. People who look like "hippies" get stopped at Customs more than average folks. Women who look like a million dollars, who are dragging their fur coats, have first-class baggage tags on their luggage and carry Gucci handbags, but declare they have bought nothing, are equally suspicious.

• Elephant ivory is illegal to import. Pieces made of ivory that are antique may be brought into the country if you have papers stating their provenance.

British Customs and Duties

EEC countries have dropped most border stipulations so it's easier to legally bring home your purchases. However, you still can't bring in any pets (at least not without a long quarantine period). You can get a VAT refund from French taxes but the paperwork and headaches involved do not pay unless you have spent a great deal of money on a single item.

CHAPTER TWO

MONEY MATTERS

Tips on Tipping

Tipping in Paris gets confusing because the basic service charges are already added to food and hotel bills and you may not always know when or what more to do. While you do not have to add onto the tip in a restaurant, it's often done—round up the bill or plunk down a few extra francs.

Figure five francs per suitcase when tipping the bellboy; two or three francs to the doorman who gets you a taxi.

Round up for taxi drivers or go to a 10% tip for big trips or airport hauls. Insist the taxi driver help you unload that luggage onto a cart before you come forward with payment and tip.

Paying Up

Whether you use cash, traveler's check or credit card, you probably are paying for your purchase in a currency different from American dollars. Airports and airplanes often take dollars anywhere in the world, and you can tip a bellboy with a one dollar bill if need be—but in France you're going to need those francs.

I think you'll do best using a credit card. Plastic is the safest to use, provides you with a record of your purchases (for U.S. Customs as well as your books) and makes returns a lot easier. Credit-card companies, because they often are associated with banks, also give the best exchange rates. You may even "make money" by charging on a credit card because the price your credit card company gives you on an exchange ratio is almost always better than what you can get for cash in a foreign country.

One thing to note about credit card charges: your purchase is posted in dollars as translated on the day your credit slip clears the credit card company (or bank) office, not the day of your purchase. If the dollar goes up in the two- or three-day lag between these two transactions, you make money; if the dollar loses strength—you pay. However, the differential is usually no more or no less than what you would suffer on the streets with a volatile exchange rate.

If you go to a shop that does not honor any of the cards you hold but does have a display of cards in the window, ask them to pull out their credit forms to find the names (and pictures) of their reciprocal bank cards. Chances are you can make a match. Access, a common European credit card, happens to be the same as Master-Card—yet this is rarely advertised.

If you happen to be given a book of discount coupons by your hotel or tour guide, you will also notice that you get a 10% discount for cash but only a 5% discount when you use credit cards. Storekeepers much prefer you to pay in cash. Remember this also when you are bargaining at the flea markets. A credit card transaction costs the retailer 2% to 5%. If you pay cash, you should be able to get that amount as a discount.

Traveler's checks are a must—for safety's sake. Shop around a bit, compare the various companies that issue checks, and make sure your checks are insured against theft or loss. I happen to use American Express traveler's checks, but they are not the only safe game in town; choose your type of check by what you can get without paying a fee. If you are a member of the AAA (American Automobile Association), you can get American Express traveler's checks without paying a fee—this alone is worth the membership dues.

I use AAA to obtain traveler's checks in foreign currency—they don't come in every currency, but they are available in French francs. You may have to order ahead. If you don't travel to France frequently, you don't want more than you can use, but a few hundred dollars worth of francs will make changing money that much easier, since you are not converting currency. Do watch the rates for a few weeks while you contemplate this purchase; once you buy you are locked into the rate.

Remember when you are trying to figure out how much things cost to divide by the rate for which you paid for your money, not the bank rate.

Currency Exchange

Changing currency in a foreign country can be downright depressing. I've taken to changing at my hotel—and buying French francs in traveler's check form before I leave town—because the time and aggravation involved in changing money in Paris can drive you nuts.

The rate announced in the paper (it's in the *Herald Tribune* every day) is the official bank exchange rate and is not usually available to tourists. Even by trading your money at a bank you will not get the same rate of exchange that's announced in the papers. And you will pay a fee for the bank's services. I've stood in lines at banks for twenty or thirty minutes to try to save $3 and realized it was a total waste of my time. I've also been to those Exchange booths that dot the Rue Rivoli and the Champs-Élysées and found that even if they advertise a great rate of exchange, there is usually a hidden hook—a $10 fee!

- You may get a better rate of exchange for a traveler's check than for cash because there is less paperwork involved for banks, hotels, etc.

- The rate of exchange you get anywhere is usually not negotiable with that establishment. While you can shop for the best rate available, you cannot haggle for a better rate from a certain source.

- Hotels generally give the least favorable rate of exchange, but they do not charge a fee for hotel guests. As far as I'm concerned, if there's no line and the people are pleasant, this is the best bet!

- Shops may negotiate on the rate of exchange. Say the item you buy costs the equivalent of $40 and you sign over a $50 U.S. traveler's check. The shopkeeper may ask you the rate of exchange, or say something like "Let's see—today the dollar is trading at..." He (or you) then will pull out a calculator and figure out how much change you will get. If you have bought a lot, you may ask for a more favorable rate of exchange on your change, or bargain a bit. Exclusive shops will be insulted at this maneuver (use credit cards there, anyway).

- Do not expect a bank to give you a better rate than your hotel because the bank usually charges a commission. If you change a check each day, expect to get a lousy rate and pay $5 per exchange.

- American Express has a flagship office (Rue Scribe) across the street from Opéra and the Le Grand Hôtel Intercontinental (one block from GALERIES LAFAYETTE)—this is a convenient place to visit and can be worthwhile since they do not charge a commission for card holders. Other services (financial and tourist) are provided as well. You certainly don't want to stop here every day to change money, but this is a good pit stop. They give the best rate in town as well.

- If you are going to Brussels and want correct change, do not change dollars in France (even at American Express) as you will be charged to change from dollars to French francs and then from French francs to Belgian francs! The American Express office even gave me Belgian money that had been out of circulation for over three years and was totally worthless. This is not particularly fun...or funny when you are on the road for a short period of time.

- If you want to change money back to dollars when you leave a country, remember that you will pay a higher rate for them. You are now "buying" dollars rather than "selling" them. Therefore, never change more money than you think you will need, unless you stockpile for another trip.

- Have some foreign currency on hand for arrivals. After a lengthy transatlantic flight, you will not want to stand in line at some airport booth just to get your cab fare. You'll pay a very high rate of exchange and be wasting your precious bathtub time. Your home bank or local currency exchange office can sell you small amounts of foreign currency. No matter how much of a premium you pay for this money, the convenience will be worth it. I get $100 worth of currency for each country I visit to have on me upon arrival; I buy it at the airport before I depart. This pays for the taxi to the hotel, tips and the immediate necessities until I decide where to change the rest of my money.

- Keep track of what you pay for your currency. If you are going to several countries, or you must make several money-changing trips to the cashier, write down the sums. When you get home and wonder what you did with all the money you used to have, it'll be easier to trace your cash. When you are budgeting, adjust to the rate you paid for the money, not the rate you read in the newspaper.

• Make mental comparative rates for quick price reactions. Know the conversion rate for $50 and $100 so that in an instant you can make a judgment. If you're still interested in an item, slow down and figure out the accurate price.

How to Get Cash Overseas

Go to American Express for quick cash. Card members may draw on their cards for cash advances or may cash personal checks. *Never travel without your checkbook.*

It's all a relatively simple transaction—you write a personal check at a special desk and show your card; it is approved; you go to another desk and get the money in the currency you request. Allow about a half hour for the whole process, unless there are long lines. Usually you get the credit advance on your card at the same desk.

BANK MACHINES

Sacré cash card! This is the start of something big and will soon be your easiest and possibly best way for changing money—*le bank machine*.

Bank cash machines are being used in Europe, but don't count on finding them everywhere you go, and don't be surprised if they won't take your card. I tried a machine in Paris and was instructed, in French, mind you:

"Please introduce your card."

I insert card.

"Your card is not remembered."

Reject.

That's not to say that a bank machine won't work for you, you just have to find the right machine to match your card. Don't leave home without the address of corresponding banks or where the proper cash machines may be located.

New ones pop up daily; you may find some as you stroll around town. The rule seems to be that when you need one you can't find one; but remember, this is the wave of the future.

Also note: American Express machines will dispense cash if you are already set up for this service.

SEND MONEY

You can have money sent to you from home, a process that usually takes about two days. Money can be wired through Western Union (someone brings them the cash or a certified check, and WU does the rest—this may take up to a week) or through an international money order, which is cleared by telex through the bank where you cash it. Money can be wired from bank to bank, but this works simply only with major banks from big cities that have European branches or sister banks. Banks usually charge a nice fat fee for doing you this favor. Call Western Union at (800) 325-6000.

If you have a letter of credit, however, and a corresponding bank that is expecting you, you will have little difficulty getting your hands on some extra green...or pink or blue or orange.

American Express can arrange for a Money Gram, a check for up to $500 that can be sent to you by family or friends at home. You then cash it at the Amex office. Call (800) 543-4080 in the U.S.

Détaxe

The *détaxe* is a 12% to 18% value-added tax that is levied on all goods, just like a sales tax in the United States. The French pay it automatically. Tourists can get a refund on it, as can visitors from other EEC countries when the tab is big enough. The amount of the tax credit varies with the type of item bought. The furniture tax is different from the luxury goods tax; and the luxury goods tax rate is falling due to pressure to re-align taxes with other EEC countries.

The basic *détaxe* system works pretty much like this:

- You are shopping in a store with prices marked on the merchandise. This is the true price of the item that any tourist or any national must pay. (This applies to stores, not flea markets.) If you are a national, you pay the price without thinking twice. If you are a tourist who plans to leave the country within six months, you may qualify for a *détaxe* refund. But wait: there's a hitch. Each store establishes the amount of money you must spend to qualify for the refund on an individual basis. You must immediately ask a salesperson, "What is the minimum expenditure in this store for the export refund?" The rate varies from shop to shop, although the minimum is set by law. Currently the *détaxe* is refunded to a person who spends between 1,000 and 1,200 French francs total in one store. Many stores let you save up receipts over a period of six months.

- Once you know the minimum, judge accordingly if you will make a smaller purchase or come back another time for a big haul...or if you will horde receipts. Only you know how much time your schedule will permit for shopping or what your bottom line budget is. Spending to save doesn't always make sense. Keep the discount in perspective.

- If you are going to another European country, consider the export tax credit policy there. For example, you probably won't get the *détaxe* in Italy. You'll get the VAT in England, it's 7.5%, and you usually need to spend only 50£ to qualify in England—but that too is flexible. (Harrod's makes you spend 150£ before you get a refund.) Balance local good buys against foreign *détaxe* credits as well. In other words, perfume is not a good buy in England so who cares if you get a VAT refund when the mark-up is much higher than in France in the first place? France or the French West Indies are absolutely the best places in the world to buy French perfume; no discount plan or VAT refund plan should dissuade you otherwise.

- If you go for the *détaxe*, budget your time to allow for the paperwork. It takes about fifteen minutes to fill out the forms, and may take twenty to sixty minutes for you to be processed if you are shopping in a big department store during the tourist season. I have zipped through in less than five minutes, so don't be frightened. But do allow more time than you need, just in case.

- You will need your passport number (but not necessarily the passport itself) for the forms. The space that asks for your address is asking for your hotel. The name of the hotel will suffice, not its entire address. (Don't be so surprised; few people know the street address of a hotel!)

- After the papers are filled in, they will be given to you along with an envelope. Sometimes the envelope has a stamp on it; sometimes it is blank (you must provide the postage stamp before you leave the country); sometimes it has a special government frank that serves as a stamp. If you don't understand what's on your envelope, ask.

- When you are leaving the country, go to the Customs official who serves the *détaxe* papers. Do this before you clear regular customs or send off your luggage. The Customs officer has the right to ask you to show him (or her) the merchandise you bought and are taking out of the country. Whether the officer sees your purchases or not, he or she will stamp the papers, keeping a set (which will be processed) and giving you another set, in the envelope. You then mail the envelope (usually it is preprinted with the shop's name and address or will have been addressed by the shop for you). The Customs officer keeps the specially franked envelopes, sometimes. Don't worry, they'll be mailed.

- When the papers get back to the shop and the government has notified the shop that their set of papers has been registered, the store will then grant you the discount through a refund. This can be done on your credit card, of which they will have made a dual pressing, or through a personal check, which will come to you in the mail, usually three months later. (It will be in a foreign currency—your bank may charge you to change it into dollars.)

OK, that's how the system works. Now here are the fine points:

The way in which you get your discount is somewhat negotiable! At the time of the purchase, discuss your options for the refund with the retailer. Depending on how much you have bought, how big a store it is, or how cute you are, you may get a more favorable situation. There are three different ways in which you can get the refund; in order of preference to the tourist they are:

1) The retailer sells you the merchandise at the cheapest price possible, including the discount, and therefore actually takes a loss on income until the government reimburses him. For example: The bottle of fragrance you want costs $50. The discount is $7.50. The best possible deal you could ever get is for the retailer to charge you $42.50 flat, give you the *détaxe* papers, and explain to you that he will not get the rest of his money unless

you process the papers properly. Being as honorable as you are, of course you process the papers. We've been offered this method at CASTY, the duty free perfume shop in the Paris Intercontinental, and at BOTTEGA VENETA.

2) Almost as simple is the credit card refund. You pay for the purchase, at the regular retail price, with a major credit card. Then your card is restamped for a refund slip, marked for the amount of the *détaxe*. You sign both slips at the time of the purchase. When the papers come back to the retailer, the shop puts through the credit slip. The credit may appear on the same monthly statement as the original bill or on a subsequent bill. Just remember to check for the credits.

3) You pay the regular retail price, with cash, traveler's check or credit card. This is the most widely-used method. You are given the forms, you go through the refund process, you get on your plane and go home. Several months later (usually about three) you get a check in the mail, made out for the refund. This check is in the currency of the country in which you made the purchase and will have to be converted to dollars and cents, a process for which your bank may charge you a percentage or a fee. Or you can go to Deak Perera or another currency broker and get the money in the currency of origin to save for your next trip to that country. Either way, it's a pain in the neck

4) A new system is sweeping EEC countries— it's run by a private company that handles VAT refunds for all tourists and is more advanced and established in other countries, but is beginning to get going in France. This system has a kiosk at the airport, so you turn in your *détaxe* paperwork—as described

above—and while you stand there in the French airport of your choice, you get the refund in the cash of your choice. That's right: dollars, francs or even yen. Look for the kiosk or ask for it—it's dressed in red, white and blue like the French flag and says "Tax Free for Tourists".

Détaxe on Trains

If you leave Paris by train—as I do frequently—you may be in a panic about your *détaxe* refund. Not to worry. Shortly after you board your international train, the conductor for your car will poke his head into your cabin, introduce himself (he speaks many languages), ask for your passport and give you the customs papers for the crossing of international borders. If you are on the sleeper, he handles the paperwork in the middle of the night while you sleep. If you have *détaxe* papers, provide them at this time. You can act nervous and fuss a bit but this guy knows exactly what to do. It is customary to provide a small tip for him when you depart anyway; if he has secured your papers you may want to add to the depth of the tip.

In all my years of doing this—I invariably take a train from Paris to Italy—I have never had to show my goods or get up in the middle of the night. It's all done without a hitch.

Driving for Détaxe

Should you be on a driving trip, or even tooling around the south of France and heading to Italy before you depart from Nice, you can get your *détaxe* paperwork stamped at the drive-through customs windows. You will have to get out of the car and stand in line, but it shouldn't take very long. You can do all your paperwork at the Nice airport, but it's nice to get rid of it.

One Last Calculating Thought

Unless you have a Ph.D. in mathematics from MIT, I suggest you keep a calculator in your purse. Furthermore, it should be the kind that uses batteries. Solar-run calculators are very cute, but your purse is dark inside, and many shops are, too. There's nothing worse than trying to do a hard bit of negotiating when your calculator won't calculate. If you use your calculator frequently, or if your children like to play with it as a toy, buy new batteries before you leave on the trip.

If you do not have a calculator with you but are contemplating a large purchase, ask the store to provide a calculator or to "run the numbers" for you. The difference between dividing by 5 and 5.3 can matter.

CHAPTER THREE

NEIGHBORHOODS

The Bastille Is Up

Paris is a city of neighborhoods. Although conveniently divided into *arrondissements*, even those neighborhoods have their own neighborhoods and those of us who prowl the streets come to categorize sections by their landmarks and their stores. OK, so the Bronx isn't up and the Battery isn't down in this town, but the way I look at it— the Bastille is uptown and the Arc de Triomphe is downtown.

Even if you live in Paris, you could never know the whole city. As a tourist, you'll probably stick to a dozen or so neighborhoods that are must-see, must-return-to areas. Some you visit just for shopping, most you wander for the combination of sights, shopping and sensations. There are streets that fulfill all your fantasies of what France should be—and these are the ones you will enjoy the most. Come with me.

The more I travel, the more I organize my time according to neighborhoods that will offer a lot of pow. I become more and more reluctant to go off on a wild-goose chase to hunt down a single address. While the city limits of Paris may sprawl all the way to the highway loop Périphérique (and beyond), my parts of town are compact and easy to manage. See Chapter Eight for specific tours; here's an overview of what's out there.

The Arrondissements

THE FIRST (1ᴱᴿ)

This neighborhood is not only known as the first, but it is also first in my heart. Although the 1ᵉʳ is one of the smallest *arrondissements*, it was not the first *arrondissement* created—so much for figuring out the reasoning behind naming these neighborhoods. Paris actually began on the Ile de la Cité, which is in the 4ᵉ. The 1ᵉʳ is a primary shopping area, with several high-rent neighborhoods and four main districts: Louvre, Halles, Palais-Royal and Vendôme (Tuileries). It is a prime shopping neighborhood because you have the fancy-dancy designer boutiques on the Rue du faubourg-Saint-Honoré (which actually crosses into the 8ᵉ) and the many wonderful boutiques on the Rue Saint-Honoré, and then you have TT (Tourist Trap) heaven along the Rue de Rivoli, and you even get the museum shop of The Louvre, a big antiques center and the Palais-Royal. I mean, this is it—Number One in my heart.

The most amazing thing about the 1ᵉʳ is the diversity of shopping. You get the wild-and-crazy, just-up-from-nothing, and still-tarnished feel of Les Halles, with its punk shops, souvenir shops and crazy boutiques; you get the Rue de Rivoli mobs that fill the department store BHV; and then you get the tourists who pour out of the Louvre near the Palais-Royal and fan down the Rue de Rivoli toward Concorde until they reach the Rue du faubourg-Saint-Honoré, one of the fanciest streets in Paris...in all Europe.

I prefer to stay in the 1ᵉʳ, so I consider it my neighborhood, the essence of my Paris. I marvel at the Rue de Rivoli on one side—so incredibly touristy—and the Rue Saint-Honoré, just on the other side, which is exactly what you came to Paris to see but which no one ever told you was there: it's a real-life neighborhood with little shops, food markets and the true feel of Paris *sans* tourists. Get back in there and prowl. And don't forget to stop at ANGELINA (page 35) for a snack, meal or hot chocolate.

THE SECOND (2ᴱ)

The 2ᵉ is called Bourse, and consists of four districts: Gaillon, Vivienne, Mail, and Bonne-Nou-velle.

You may not find yourself here too much unless you have the heart of a *garmento* and want to visit the Sentier, which is the garment center and has tons of little wholesale-only shops where, if you have nerve, you can ask if they'll sell to you. (Many will.) The GALERIE VIVIENNE is in the 2ᵉ, although its charm is fading with yearly graffiti and lack of attention. Essentially the 2ᵉ is very businessy and wholesaley—not that charming a place (with exceptions, of course).

Note: Victoires is on the border of the 1ᵉʳ and 2ᵉ, and it is one of the highlights of Paris because of its designer and avant-garde shops. Also note that the kitchen supply houses (page 198) are in the 2ᵉ. All in all, the 2ᵉ has a good bit to offer.

THE THIRD (3ᴱ)

Nicknamed either Temple or Marais, the 3ᵉ has become popular with the renaissance of the Marais itself and the Place des Vosges (which happens to be on the border of the 3ᵉ and 4ᵉ)—and is a must-do, must-drool on your tour of Paris.

The opening of the Picasso Museum, which is in the 3ᵉ but near the 4ᵉ, and the rebirth of the Place des Vosges (4ᵉ) brought in many tourists, and cute shops have blossomed like rosebuds. There's also a big covered market called the Car-reau du Temple, where you can find old clothes (*fripes*) and some nice handcrafted items. It's open every day except Monday; no designer clothes here. Don't get mixed up between Rue du Temple and Boulevard du Temple.

Boulevard du Temple and that part of the neighborhood backs up to République, and this is a very middle-class, working-class kind of neighborhood that has a good number of discounters and rather shabby outlets that probably aren't worth investigating—and certainly aren't worth your time if you are a Rue du faubourg-Saint-Honoré kind of customer.

THE FOURTH (4E)

This neighborhood backs up on the Marais and the Place des Vosges—which is a very grand and wonderful place to live. At one end it borders on the 3e at the Place des Vosges. Not far away there is a famous and very colorful old Jewish neighborhood. The Village Saint Paul (antiques galore) is here; you are a stone's throw from Bastille, which is lacking the fortress of your childhood imagination but does have the fortress of the new opera house. Once you cross the Boulevard Bourdon at the canal you are in the 12e, but never mind. There is the Brocante de Bastille every April, held along the banks of the canal, which is a sensational flea market, even if you do have to pay admission. Also note the 4e includes the Ile Saint-Louis; the local church is the Cathedral of Notre Dame.

THE FIFTH (5E)

This is the famous Latin Quarter, or student quarter, which is also called Panthéon. *C'est la Bohème*—it's filled with little *cafés* and restaurants; it's paradise for book-hunters. There are shops selling *fripes* and jeans, as that seems to be all that people around here wear. There's a large American population in this quarter, and a large Muslim population near the mosque. Open markets are at Carmes, Place Maubert, on Tuesday, Thursday and Saturday, as well as at Port-Royal on the same days. The Sunday market is at Place Monge.

THE SIXTH (6^E)

One of the most Parisian *arrondissements* for tourists and shoppers, the 6e is called Luxembourg because of the gardens by the same name, or Saint-Germain-des-Prés because of the church and main drag of the same name. The street market on the Rue de Buci, with the fruits, vegetables and flowers piled high, is a sight for a photographer. The antiques business is clustered here, as is the one-of-a-kind boutique business. This remains one of Paris' most vibrant and exciting shopping districts; many of Hemingway's favorite *cafés* and haunts are here; you can sit at an expensive sidewalk *café*, watch Paris walk by and have the time of your life.

THE SEVENTH (7^E)

An expensive area for shopping, it's also known as Palais-Bourbon, and districts include: Saint-Thomas-d'Aquin, Invalides, École Militaire, and Gros-Caillou.

There is an open market on Thursday and Saturday in Breteuil at the Avenue de Saxe, a covered market in Gros-Caillou on the Rue Jean-Nicot.

The real news is for foodies: the Rue Cler reigns as the street for food, serious food. Foodies from all over the world work this two-block street, take notes, taste everything and discuss their finds for years. The main shopping streets are Rue de Grenelle (which is also partially in the 6e) and Rue Saint-Dominique. There are many small shops for rich ladies who just can't go so far as the crass Rue du faubourg-Saint-Honoré or the crasser Champs-Élysées. And yes, the Tour Eiffel is in the 7e.

THE EIGHTH (8^E)

Élysées is the 8e, which stretches right across some of the best shopping in the world and is nestled between the 1er and the 16e. One of my favorite shopping jaunts is to walk across these three *arrondissements* in a more or less straight line from the Hôtel Meurice along the Rue du faubourg-Saint-Honoré to Place de l'Alma at the end of Avenue Montaigne. Avenue Montaigne has recently become the fanciest retail street in Paris, and is far more upscale than the Rue du faubourg-Saint-Honoré these days. This is a bit of a walk but not an impossible one, unless you are loaded down with shopping bags.

THE NINTH (9^E)

The 9e is famous to most of the world as Opéra. This is where GALERIES LAFAYETTE, MONOPRIX, and AU PRINTEMPS, as well as PRISUNIC, MARKS & SPENCER and every street vendor in Paris are gathered in the most concentrated area of shopping per meter you'll find in Paris. It's a bit of a zoo, but it's fun. You can see a lot (and buy a lot) in a short period of time. American Express also is in this neighborhood, if you need more money. And frankly, who doesn't? Remember the *métro* at Chaussée-d'Antin; it is your key in and out of the 9e. The RER stop is at Opéra but it's called Auber (half a block from Opéra)—this is where you get the train to EuroDisney. Le Grand Hôtel Intercontinental is right here. My personal grocery store of the area is located above Monoprix—it's owned by Galeries Lafayette; I think it's more fun than FAUCHON.

THE TENTH (10^E)

Wholesale, did you say you like wholesale? Well, the 10^e is one of the many wholesale neighborhoods—this one is for furs, glass, china and coiffure suppliers. The Saint-Denis area is filled with hookers, hoods and dealers. It has a strong ethnic mix as well. Not one of your must-see, must-write-home-about areas. Both the Gare du Nord and the Gare de l'Est are in the 10^e as is the Rue de Paradis—a street filled with shops selling glass and china and crystal and yes, those little

Limoges boxes Carolyn loves. While the Saint Denis area is a little dicey, the area around the train stations and the Rue de Paradis is perfectly safe in the day. By night, there are a lot of famous jazz clubs. But they don't have stores.

THE ELEVENTH (11^E)

République is a middle-class neighborhood. There are some discounters, but mostly this is not a neighborhood you would go out of your way to shop in, simply because there is little that is special here. The furniture business stretches along the Rue du faubourg-Saint-Antoine, but it's not the kind of furniture you're looking for.

THE TWELFTH (12^E)

This is Bastille–Gare de Lyon, and sits on the other side of the 4^e, across the canal. The districts are Bastille, Nation (partly in 20^e), Reuilly and Daumesnil. Nation is for real people, but Bastille is getting very hot for *artistes*.

Tons of American artists (as well as others) live here; the area is quite hip. This is a very large *arrondissement* with a lot of different neighborhoods: what you get around the Place du Bastille is very different from what you get down the street at Ledru-Rollin (JEAN-LOUIS SCHERRER outlet store) and dramatically different from other sections of the same *arrondissement*. Except for a few choice spots, this is not really tourist territory.

It is design, art gallery and furniture territory. Check out the Rue de Charrone as well as the Rue du faubourg-Saint-Antoine for furniture and decorative arts shops. There are many galleries on the Rue Keller and a few on the Rue de Lappe. For gallery hoppers, stand with the Bastille *métro* station to your back or take the exit for Rue de la Roquette. Follow it away from Bastille (your only choice) go one block, hang a right on the Rue du Lappe. Hang a left on the Rue du Charonne and then another left on Rue de Keller. *Voilà*—you've seen it all.

On the other hand, for the bargain hunters, a not-so-touristy but terrific place is the Place d'Aligre: a fun French adventure. The open market (Beauvau-Saint-Antoine) is at the Place d'Aligre, which is open every day except Monday until 1 P.M. and backs up to the covered market of the same name. The streets are filled with vendors selling fruit and veggies, flowers and *fripes*. It's a very "real people" neighborhood, not at all glamorous or quaint. But it's intensely French. There's a supermarket here if you want to buy a *picnique* from the vendors and finish it off at the market. BETTY (page 105) is a well-known discounter who sells suits as well as fabrics from Léonard.

THE THIRTEENTH (13^E)

One of the largest *arrondissements* of Paris, the 13e is mostly residential and of little interest to tourists; part of the area is known as the French Chinatown. The districts are Italie, Gobelins and Austerlitz. You can pass.

THE FOURTEENTH (14^E)

A SONIA RYKIEL outlet store? Step this way. The 14e is home to the Rue d'Alésia, a street of several bargain shops. There's also a great flea market here (Place de Vanves). Montparnasse is here if it interests you—in all its high-rise, Los Angeles-style glory. The neighborhood is large and has many districts—some are nice, others are not. But the *stock* shops and the flea market should by your primary reasons to visit the 14^e.

THE FIFTEENTH (15^E)

Fashion groupies of the world, unite: The 15^e is yours if you come to Paris for *prêt*, or if you like to do half a day's bargain shopping. The Porte de Versailles is here, and there are tons of commercial streets all around. Rue de la Convention is a main drag. Mostly this is a middle-class neighborhood; if you don't have business here, it's unlikely you'll stop by.

THE SIXTEENTH (16E)

To many Parisians there is only one *arrondisse-ment* in Paris, and its number is 16. The districts are Auteuil, Passy, Chaillot, Muette, and Porte Dauphine.

It just so happens that there are a few parts of the 16e that aren't chic (e.g., Port de Saint-Cloud), but this is the seat of the BCBG (*bon chic, bon genre*), the FHCP (Foulard-Hermès-Collier-de Perles), and the Nappy Society (named for the proper neighborhoods Neuilly, Auteuil, and Passy). What more could a yuppie want? Rue de Passy is the best commercial stretch of residential Paris. The 16e has its own park, the B*ois*, and it's very chic to live close to the park. More important, the 16e has lots of resale shops. The 8th and the 16th bump heads over couture shopping. Ooh la la.

THE SEVENTEENTH (17E)

It's OK, M*aman* won't disown you if you live in the 17e (or parts of it, anyway). The acceptable districts for the BCBG group are Péreire, Ternes and Monceau.

THE EIGHTEENTH (18E)

You know the 18e because it includes the Montmartre neighborhood. Other districts in it are Clignancourt, Pigalle, Chapelle and Goutte-d'Or. This is a very scenic part of Paris, a part that tourists like to visit in order to see if their fantasies about Paris are true, and is also the site of some of the fabric markets that design students haunt. Of course, all students of shopping know that Clignancourt means flea market in French. (Well, sort of.)

While the 18e was charming and famous and really cute for movies (*Irma la Douce*), books (*Mistral's Daughter*) and tourists (up to twenty years ago, anyway), now it is a less-than-charming place. The fabric markets of Saint-Pierre are near Sacré-Coeur.

THE NINETEENTH (19^E)

This really is getting out of the swing of things; as you get to the Villette part of this *arrondissement* you are at the edge of the highway that encompasses Paris. There's no shopping reason to visit.

THE TWENTIETH (20^E)

Maurice Chevalier made the area famous when he sang about Ménilmontant, but other than that there isn't too much going on in this residential neighborhood inhabited by people who can't afford high rents in other parts of town. The famous Père-Lachaise cemetery is here; the only piece of retailing advice I have regarding the cemetery is to make sure you buy a map of the gravestones; otherwise you will never find Jim Morrison's.

Shopping Neighborhoods

Luckily for a visitor to the sprawling city of Paris, the prime shopping is concentrated in a few neighborhoods, and despite the fact that many new stores come on board each year, the really good ones are smart enough to open in existing high-traffic areas. The neighborhoods below are not listed in any order of shopping preference (they are divided by the Seine, however); there is some deference to personal fantasies and tourist timetables. Let's face it: everyone wants to go to Notre Dame. You may as well know how to shop your way there.

Right Bank

Shopping opportunities on the Right Bank are not as dense as on the Left Bank—it'll take you several days to do justice to the 6^e—but the major shopping on the Left Bank is conveniently located in one *arrondissement*. While I'd be happy to tell you the major shopping of the Right Bank is in the 1er, that's not really accurate. For those who only have a short period of time in Paris and who might want to hit the big department stores on the Boulevard Haussmann—it could be that all the shopping choices you'll need are in the 9th. So get out your marking pen and underline, draw stars and fix notes to those places that sound like your cup of tea. Many of the stores mentioned are discussed in more depth later in the book.

CHAMPS-ÉLYSÉES

I will tell you right up front in my all-too-American way, if you skip the Champs-Élysées, it's OK with me. The charm is mostly (but not completely) gone. The first vision a schoolchild has of Paris usually includes the wide boulevard of the Champs-Élysées, crowned by L'Étoile and the Arc de Triomphe. *Dommage*. The old girl just ain't what she used to be. I like to walk right past it on my way elsewhere with perhaps just a quick stop by PRISUNIC, the best French variety dime store, or the VIRGIN MEGASTORE, which is either the beginning of the new world or the end of the old world and has to be seen to be appreciated. I'd say twenty minutes in Virgin and another twenty minutes in Prisunic and you've done the Champs-Élysées. And if you pride yourself on your matching Louis Vuitton luggage, neither of these places will interest you much.

Should you decide to tackle the Champs-Élysées despite my opinions to the contrary, here's your best shot: start at Rond Point. If you are standing at the Rond Point and looking straight ahead to the Arc de Triomphe, the good side of the street for shopping is on your right. You can begin at the YSL ROND POINT or the shopping gallery called GALERIE-ÉLYSÉES ROND POINT, which is a rather modern shopping mall not unlike one in your home city, except that it has only sixteen shops.

Along the way you'll see numerous car showrooms, perfume showrooms, drugstores, airlines offices, *cafés*, and change booths. A few big-name designers have stores here, such as DANIEL HECHTER and TON SUR TON. GALERIE DU CLARIDGE has two levels (go downstairs, too) and has the best selection among the kind of shops you want to see—most of them are big-name designers.

In two big blocks you'll be at PRISUNIC. If you travel with your children, don't miss this location for cheap clothes, cheap toys and the grocery store on the downstairs level.

If time is precious, you might want to knock off here and dart into the Franklin D. Roosevelt *métro* station right near Prisunic. If you want a taxi, you cannot hail one. Taxis congregate in the center of the street in a taxi island; just signal to one and it will come to you.

If you want a quick snack, there are millions of choices—from fast food to the somewhat famous. I stick to pizza at MAMA MIA, right off the Champs-Élysées on Rue Marbeuf.

AVENUE MONTAIGNE

Now we're talking! You want the real Paris that dreams are made of? You want stores that are drop-dead fancy, where the women who patronize them wear couture and carry little doggies under their arms? Little doggies with couture hair ribbons, right? You want architecture and trees with little lights in them and even a view of the Tour Eiffel. *Ici*. Madame, you have arrived.

The Avenue Montaigne has heretofore been a very nice street in Paris; one of the nicest, in fact. Now it has become a monument to itself. Beginning with the French Bicentennial celebrations (of the retail sort), and continuing today, the street has become the fanciest address in town and a destination unto itself. Changes on the Rue du faubourg-Saint-Honoré have made it less desirable to the really fancy retailers; a not-so-subtle shift has transformed the formerly laid-back Avenue Montaigne from secretly elegant to seriously grand. CHRISTIAN DIOR and NINA RICCI have always been here; the CHANEL boutique was sort of a secret to those in the know, because out-of-towners stick to the Rue Cambon address, but locals use this one. The arrival of LOUIS VUITTON and their glitzy flagship store heralded the change, and now ESCADA has climbed on board with INES DE LA FRESSANGE following suit in her Henri Bendel-look-alike salon. One stroll down the two blocks of retail in this short street will give you a look at these famous names as well as HAREL (for gorgeous shoes), THIERRY MUGLER, EMANUEL UNGARO, PORTHAULT, CÉLINE, CHRISTIAN LACROIX and VALENTINO. Some of the non-designer type stores are old-fashioned French shops that deserve a visit just to soak up atmosphere; try AU DUC DE PRASLIN (a candy and nuts store) and PARFUMS CARON with its giant glass bottles filled with perfumes.

You can get here by walking over from the Champs-Élysées (try Rond Point for the low approach, or Franklin Roosevelt for the high approach), or by emerging from the Alma Marceau *métro* station right at the far end of Avenue Montaigne. In that case, you'll walk toward the Champs-Élysées. Walk both sides of the street and arrive back at Alma Marceau, where you can hang a left at the Place de l'Alma and follow the signs to the *bateaux-mouche,* Paris' famous boat rides. Don't miss a chance to take tea at the HÔTEL PLAZA ATHÉNÉE or to eat at CHEZ FRANCIS—a rather typical neighborhood bistro—both are right there on Avenue Montaigne.

FAUBOURG-SAINT-HONORÉ

And while I'm still hot on how much the Champs-Élysées has changed, let me also add that the faubourg-Saint-Honoré has also gone downhill. As you already know, the Rue du faubourg-Saint-Honoré is known simply as the faubourg—and is *the* place for the fanciest antiques dealers and the high-end designers. While the street is still dense with the best names in both businesses, there's lots of comings and goings, and a subtext that is slightly *déclassé*. The anointed have moved to Avenue Montaigne.

Sure, the neighborhood is still fun. You cannot come to Paris and not stop by, not visit HERMÈS. (Or CARITA, see page 174) But it has suffered from recession and maybe from excess, and furthermore, I don't believe in wasting my precious Paris shopping time at stores that are too rich for my blood. After you've done your thing on the faubourg, segue right onto the plain old Rue Saint-Honoré. Now that's my kind of place.

SAINT-HONORÉ

This is not on your typical list of Paris neighborhoods because you probably don't know it exists, or you think it's part of the faubourg, even though it's not. This is my secret Paris: From the Hôtel du Louvre, where it is funky and neighborhoody, to the Rue Castiglione where it begins to get hoity-toity, to the Rue Royale where it becomes super fancy and eventually turns into the Rue du faubourg-Saint-Honoré designation. Plenty of designer shops are located in the Castiglione area (LAURA ASHLEY, MCM, LACOSTE) but the area also offers plenty of mom-and-pop retailers. The farther you get from the Rue Royale, the more casual the neighborhood gets—be sure to wander onto the tiny Place du Marché Saint-Honoré, which leads to the market as well as a number of little shops, some designer (MODEL, CASTALBAJAC) and some would-be, as well as several food shops and groceries. My neighborhood pizza place is PIZZERIA VENUS (#326). Get a look at shops like BIBERON & FILS (#334) which is actually an office supply store that might not interest you if you were merely window-shopping. Stand far enough back in the street to get a look at the entire storefront—it is preserved just as it was in 1836 and is often featured in postcards, movies and photos.

If you're out on a stroll, take the Rue Saint-Honoré to the Comédie Français. Here you can hang a right and go to the Louvre; or left and shop in the arcades at the Palais-Royal (DIDIER LUDOT) and then move right along to Victoires and the 2e. Or you can hit the Rue de Rivoli and circle back toward Concorde while you visit all the TT's...and Angelina.

VICTOIRES

If you want to have a wonderful shopping experience that's very French and very special head for Place des Victoires—which is nestled back into the area behind the Palais-Royal where the 1er and the 2^e connect. The Place des Victoires is a plaza complete with a statue of a king on a horse. Facing the *place* is a circle of hotels; the ground floor of each has been converted to retail space. The spokes of streets shooting out of the *place* represent various retail streets as well, and they are filling up with more and more wonderful shops. Rue Étienne-Marcel is the major drag—it has long housed some of the big *créateurs*. Going the other way is the Rue des Petits-Champs, which has a lot of showrooms and charming shops on it. (The GALERIE VIVIENNE is on the Rue des Petits-Champs right before the Place des Victoires.)

There's KENZO and CACHAREL and ESPRIT, but you will enjoy simply going door-to-door around the circle and then branching out down the little streets. CHEVIGNON GIRL is the teen store from the big chain Chevignon; you'll see young, kicky fashions here. Some may even be affordable. Don't miss HENRY COTTONS, an Italian, Ralph Lauren-weekend-chic sort of space with great architecture. Although the address is written as Place des Victoires, the entrance is on the Rue Étienne-Marcel.

Rue Étienne-Marcel has tons of shops and even more shopping adventures—there's CHEVIGNON TRADING POST for American country and Santa Fe-style gifts and housewares, JUNKO SHIMADO for hot fashion with hot price tags; there's a ticket shop for the museums of Paris across the street; here you can get admission tickets to the big exhibits in town without having to schlep to the museum and come back yet another time (MUSÉE & COMPAGNIE, 49 Rue Étienne-Marcel).

Don't forget to check your trusty map before you leave Victoires; because the location is so superb, you can continue in any number of directions. You can easily walk to the FORUM DES HALLES or to Opéra or the Boulevard Haussmann and the big department stores. You can also come around toward the Louvre, hit the Galerie Vivienne, then walk through the row of little shops at the Palais-Royal and hit LE LOUVRE DES ANTIQUAIRES and then the Louvre itself, its museum shop and finally the souvenir shops along the Rue de Rivoli—ending up at Concorde, or Place Vendôme, or on the Rue du faubourg-Saint-Honoré. The world starts at Victoires, and it's a magnificent world.

SENTIER

Some people have printer's ink in their veins; I've got garment center in my blood. If you do too, you may want to go from Victoires into the Sentier. From Place des Victoires, follow Rue D'Aboukir which leads you from the 1er into the 2e. Be forewarned: The Sentier may not be your kind of place: It's very much like New York's Seventh Avenue—men with pushcarts piled high with fabric, little showrooms that may or may not let you buy from them, hookers in certain doorways, junk in bins, metal racks and forklifts and hangers and mannequins without arms and all that stuff. There are few big-name designer names here, and there are no guarantees that you will find what you want. Follow the Rue D'Aboukir until it hits the Rue Montmartre then hang a right. This will give you more *garmento* stops as well as MENDÈS, the YSL outlet store, and all the kitchen stores as well. You'll end up at the FORUM DES HALLES. Any time you want to buy something, simply play dumb American: ask the price and see what happens.

One announcement: For the most part, the area is closed tight on weekends. A few shops are open on Saturday, but Saturday is not the day to tour the neighborhood and see it all. Sunday is totally dead.

If you're not sure about exploring this neighborhood in depth, you may want to walk from Place des Victoires on the Rue Étienne-Marcel which will give you a chance to take in both designer shops (see page 119) and some wholesale and *garmento* places and land you right at the Rue Montmartre for more *garmento* shopping before you move on to the mall Forum Des Halles and the Beaubourg. You'll also get the wholesale kitchen stores on this route (see page 198).

RUE DE RIVOLI

The Rue de Rivoli is the main drag that runs along the back side of the Louvre. Since the Louvre once was a fortress, you will understand why it seems to go on forever. They just don't build them like that anymore. Exit the *métro* at Concorde. The Rue de Rivoli has many chic shops on it, including LANVIN 2, the men's sports shop, and HILDITCH & KEY. As you pass the Meurice, you'll see more touristy stores, and the farther you go away from Concorde, the more touristy the stores will get. Just because a lot of tourists shop here doesn't mean this is a bad shopping area. Pick and choose at your own discretion. It sort of ends at LE LOUVRE DES ANTIQUAIRES, but the street itself—Rue de Rivoli—continues forever and has many stores on it. By the time you get up near the Hôtel de Ville, there's the giant department store BHV, which has a basement filled with gadgets for the home. But it's quite a walk from Concorde to Hôtel de Ville. Better to stop when you get to the Louvre. While you're shopping, don't forget to hop into the Louvre gift shop right under the glass pyramid.

There happen to be a number of perfume/cosmetics/duty free shops in this stretch of territory, some are rather famous. My best secret is the PARFUMERIE CHAMPS-ÉLYSÉES, which is not on the Champs-Élysées at all; try 8 Rue Royale, a stone's throw from the Concorde *métro* stop. (See page 172.)

PLACE VENDÔME

If you're looking for a neighborhood that says "Paris" and reminds you with every breath that they don't make 'em like this anymore, get yourself over to the Place Vendôme, conveniently located between Opéra and Rue de Rivoli.

Formerly one of the finest residential areas in Paris, the Place Vendôme is surrounded by old hotels that now house either jewelry shops, banks, insurance companies or all three. There's also a hotel of the type you spend the night in— the Ritz. Besides the big jewelry firms, like VAN CLEEF & ARPELS, some ready-to-wear kings have moved in—like GIORGIO ARMANI, NATORI and even Armani's EMPORIO.

The far side of the Place Vendôme is the Rue de la Paix, which dead-ends into Opéra. There are more jewelers here (and even a BURMA if you like to buy copies of what you have just seen), and a few other retailers. Don't confuse CHARVET (a men's store) with CHAUMET—a jeweler. Most exciting newcomer is PALOMA PICASSO. The American Express office is on Rue Scribe, right beside Opéra. How convenient.

HAUSSMANN

On the other side of the Opéra, and on the other side of the world from Place Vendôme, is the Boulevard Haussmann, where several department stores have their headquarters. This three-block-long and two-block-deep jumble of merchandise, pushcarts, strollers and shoppers is a central trading area. I frequently call it The Zoo. If you insist on seeing it, go early in the morning (10 A.M.), when you are strong. Winter is far less zoo-like than summer. Also note LAFAYETTE GOURMET is the grocery store attached to GALERIES LAFAYETTE—it's fabulous. This is the day you should eat at CAFÉ DE LA PAIX, although there is also a McDonald's not far away.

ROYALE

If you've had it with the Haussmann commercial area, don't want to gather your *picnique* from the GL grocery store or eat fast food from the street vendors and *crêpes* makers, you can head to FAUCHON and its stand-up cafeteria. Boulevard Haussmann hits the Rue Tronchet a block after the string of department stores, hang a left to take you two blocks to the Place de la Madeleine where Fauchon and many other food landmarks are located. Finish up here and continue on the Rue Royale leading to either the faubourg (turn right at GUCCI if the Madeleine is to your back if you want the faubourg) or Place Concorde. It's lined with big-name stores including RALPH LAUREN/POLO and all the showrooms for the glass and porcelain shops. In-between these two you'll find the modern mini-mall at LES TROIS QUARTIES where there was once a big department store. Now there's branches of KENZO, WEILL, CHACOK, BODY SHOP, MARINA RINALDI, BURMA, DOROTHÉE BIS, AGATHA, MONDI, GEORGES RECH, RODIER HOMME, STÉPHANE KELIAN and a huge perfume shop called SILVER MOON.

PASSY

The main commercial street of one of the nicest districts of one of the nicest *arrondissements* and is convenient to other neighborhoods; you can visit Passy and go on your way to the Tour Eiffel, to Trocadéro or to the resale shops of the 16e, or you can catch the *métro* and be anywhere else in minutes. Passy is in transition and seems like it fades a little every year, but it has some old faithfuls tucked between the overly commercial shops and offers an excellent chance to see some of the real Paris. Try FRANCK ET FILS (swanky department store) and SEPHORA, a cosmetics supermarket that will make you swoon. Don't miss INNO, a small *hypermarché*, for food, clothes and some gifts. PRISUNIC also has a branch on Passy. This is a fun, let's-pretend-neighborhood: you can stroll the street and pretend you are part of the French upper middle class.

BASTILLE

Don't look now, but Bastille is getting to be chic. Dare I say it? People are losing their heads over this up-and-coming neighborhood! A tad too far uptown for general retail, Bastille is benefiting from the rebirth of the Marais, one *arrondissement* over, and the ugly, but renowned, new opera house. The artists have moved in; so have the Americans (to live, not to set up shop). Long known as the basic home furnishings area, the district is now taking on some galleries and interior design shops of note. For a snack, a meal or even a take-out dinner, stop at the long-famous *brasserie*, BOFINGER, at 5 Rue de la Bastille. To see it all, take the *métro* to Ledru-Rollin and walk along the Rue du faubourg-Saint-Antoine toward the column in the center of the Place de la Bastille. This gives you the real-people view. If you want more glamour, walk along the river quais, then cut in toward the Opéra along Boulevard Bourdon, which is residential. This is where you'll find the Brocante de Bastille every April. Don't forget that there's the JEAN-LOUIS SCHERRER discount shop nearby. On the other side of the *place*, pass Bofinger and move to the Rue Saint-Antoine (the uptown name for this part of the Rue de Rivoli) where there are some discount houses. You can follow the signs to the Place des Vosges from here, you can visit the antiques market around Saint Paul or you can walk straight to the Hôtel de Ville and BHV.

MARAIS/PLACE DES VOSGES

The rebirth of the Marais is not such news these days, but new shops are still showing up, so the area becomes a pleasure to explore each time you visit Paris. Take the *métro* to Saint Paul and follow the signs. For basic lay of the land directions, the area between church of Saint Paul and the Seine hosts the Village Saint Paul for antiques; the Marais lies nestled behind the other side of the Rue Saint-Antoine and is hidden from view as you emerge from the *métro*. You will find no hint of charm until you get back from the street.

If you love the out-of-the-way and special, stay at the PAVILLON DE LA REINE which is built where the former queen's chambers once were, in the style of the 14th century—it's a true find. Take in designer shops like POPY MORENI or ISSEY MIYAKE in an arcade around the actual place. The side streets are dense with opportunities: ROMEO GIGLI, AZZEDINE ALAÏA, and CHEVIGNON with its American country looks.

As you exit the cute shopping area, you're near the Rue de Turenne—which has absolutely no charm whatsoever and may ruin the mood, but does have a ton of jobbers and discount shops (don't miss BIDERMANN, #114)—and the Rue du Temple, which is another street of discounters. In-between the two are quaint little streets and shops you've never heard of before that will bring a smile to your face and your pocketbook.

If you're looking for something unique, try ANDRÉ BISSONÉT (6 Rue du Pas-de-la-Mule), who has an amazing collection of antique musical instruments; À LA BONNE RENOMMÉE (26 Rue Vieille du Temple), which sells very expensive patchwork fashions; and AUTOUR DU MONDE (12 Rue des Francs Bourgeois), which is the French version of Banana Republic! Continuing on Rue des Francs Bourgeois, there's LEFAX (#32) for Filofax goodies in French right nearby and MONIC, for glitzy fun jewelry (#5). The most famous neighborhood hangout is MARIAGE FRERES, 30–32 Rue du Bourg Tibourg, with store, lunch and tearoom: they've been in business since 1854.

Left Bank

To many, the essence of Paris is the 6e, the Left Bank. I see it a neighborhood of several different villages nestled together—all with differing personalities. If you're the type who just likes to wander, go there and spend the day. No, just stay there and spend a week. Hmm—maybe you'd better move there. If your time is precious, perhaps you'd like to use my method of coping. After all, Gaul may be divided into three parts, but I've divided this area of one *arrondissement* into several: Saint-Germain Main, Behind the Church, Rennes Central, Mabillon, and Little Dragons. There's also Uptown Odéon, but that's another story. (See page 81.)

SAINT-GERMAIN MAIN

The main drag of the left bank is the Boulevard Saint-Germain; the center of the universe of this neighborhood is the church Saint-Germain-des-Prés. Have a taxi drop you here (or take the *métro*, no sweat) and you have arrived in the center of all the action. You can begin the day with breakfast coffee and *croissants* at any number of famous bistros from CAFÉ DEUX MAGOT, CAFÉ DE

FLORE to LE DRUGSTORE PUBLIS (not quite a
bistro but an institution nonetheless). Those who
could afford the rent on this main drag have their
stores clustered around here; pick from SONIA
RYKIEL to SHU UEMURA (a fabulous Japanese
cosmetics firm). There are several bookstores,
artsy postcard and poster shops and zillions of
cafés, since this is the heart of the dream. While
the price of your *café au lait* may be a tad higher
than around the corner, you may sit here for
hours for the price of one coffee. At night there
are often street vendors; bookstores stay open
late.

BEHIND THE CHURCH

My favorite part of the 6th is located behind
the church of Saint-Germain-des-Prés. Behind the
church you'll find Place de Furstemberg, Rue de
Buci, Rue Jacob, Rue Bonaparte, Rue de Seine,
Rue du Bac and Quai Voltaire. Many of these
streets house antiques and decorating shops; the
Rue de Buci offers a street market (open Sundays!) where flowers and food are sold in profu-
sion. This is a must-do Paris stop; let those who
appreciate a visual scene come feast their eyes.
The rest of the area is to die for as well: winding
narrow streets, tiny storefronts, windows you feel
compelled to press your nose to.

These streets are filled mostly with boutiques,
bakeries, eateries, markets and—the fame of the
neighborhood—antiques and design showrooms
(see page 205). It is very quaint back here, and the
stores feel different from the ones in the other
parts of the Left Bank. This is one of the most
charming areas in all of Paris.

RENNES CENTRAL

Across the street from the church there's LE
DRUGSTORE PUBLIS which I mention all the time
because I not only eat here a lot, but I use it as a
basic landmark. Here two streets converge in a
V—the Rue de Rennes and the Rue Bonaparte.

Bonaparte runs behind the church as well (but I am not talking about that part of Bonaparte—we are now on another side of the street); Rennes does not.

Rennes is the central drag of this trading area, which includes such streets as Rue de Seine, Rue de Tournon, Rue Saint-Sulpice, Rue Coëtlogon and Boulevard Raspail. Bonaparte, a very nice street for strolling and one you will enjoy, is sort of smaller and runs off at an angle. It feels neighborhoody; Rennes feels big city. Closer to Boulevard Saint-Germain, but on Rennes, there are many big-name designer shops from CÉLINE to CONRAN'S HABITAT, as well as GUY LAROCHE, STEFANEL, COURRÈGES, KENZO, BURBERRYS and then a number of hot-shot boutiques (LOFT) and a few real-people places as well—there's UNIPRIX, a Kmart-like department store as well as a new FNAC (records, tapes, books) etc. The deal with Rennes is that you will be tempted to quit after a block or so, but I suggest you hang on for another block or two because those who couldn't afford to take space closer to Saint-Germain have opened shop and there are a few finds to find. I'll take GENVIEVE LETHU for tabletop and fresh color and fabric ideas. The classy stuff certainly ends by the time you get to the Rue Saint-Placide, but here you have a street filled with designer discount stores (see page 82) and a way to walk right back into the heart of the area. Walk along Saint-Placide till you get to the Rue de Sèvres, then take time out for the Little Dragons area (see below) or head back over to the heart of Rennes Central and head for Mabillon.

LITTLE DRAGONS

To the right of Rennes Central (if your back is to the church) are several very small, narrow streets crammed with good things to eat and to wear. They are epitomized by the Rue du Dragon, the heart of this area, which is why I call this neighborhood Little Dragons. Also check out Rue de Grenelle and Rue des Saints-Pères. This whole warren of tiny streets is crammed with great shops, many belonging to designers of fame and fortune (FERRAGAMO, SONIA RYKIEL ENFANT, PHILIPPE MODEL). The area is clustered around the Sèvres-Babylon *métro* stop, which is a block from AU BON MARCHÉ, one of Paris' biggest and most famous department stores. This store has a fabulous grocery store as well as a level of antiques dealers in a little indoor flea market. You can also easily walk to Saint-Placide, as mentioned above, or see page 82.

MABILLON

I consider the two blocks from Rennes Central to the *métro* stop Mabillon as one area. The core of the area is between the Rue Bonaparte and the Place de Saint-Sulpice which comes complete with gorgeous church, little park, several YVES SAINT-LAURENT SHOPS and some picture postcard places. It's also full of cute stores; many are small designer shops, some with names you've heard of—like SOULEIADO, which translates to "Pierre Deux" in English. There's also representatives of the big time like MAX MARA, and still others are trendy today and maybe gone tomorrow. Don't miss the Rue Bonaparte; it's part of what you came to Paris to see.

UPTOWN ODÉON

This area is adjacent to Mabillon, just a little further up, and ends at the Boulevard Saint-Michel. The designer and chic shopping begins to peter out; this is more of a funky student area. As a result, there are tons of good bookstores including a giant GILBERT JEUNE bookstore at the corner of Boulevard Saint-Michel, and if you are walking on to Notre Dame you can head up this way and pass these sights—or you can walk along the quai and shop the stalls that sell postcards (old and new), prints, botanicals, old magazines and books.

Discount Neighborhoods

ALÉSIA

Pronounced "Aleeeza" by some and "heaven" by others, this is one of the major discount districts in Paris. Prices in some of these shops may not be the lowest possible, but there are a good half dozen shops to choose from.

Tip: Not every store in this area is a discount house, so ask if you are confused. Don't make any false assumptions! Most of the discount houses have the word *stock* in their name, which means they sell overruns. There are three such *stock* shops for DOROTHÉE BIS (at #74, 76, and 78 Rue d'Alésia), and then there's one of my faves, STOCK 2, a warehouse kind of place that feels as nice as a department store, which sells men's, women's and kids' designer clothes at discount prices. Most of it is from Daniel Hechter, but there are other brands. Don't miss CACHAREL STOCK with fabulous baby and kids' clothes as well as men's and women's things. Highlight of the block is undoubtedly SR (# 64 Rue d'Alésia) which stands for, shout it out folks, Sonia Rykiel.

SAINT-PLACIDE

This is not particularly near Alésia (although you can walk from one area to the other), but mentally the two areas are sisters—homes of the discount shop, the *stock* shop, the great bargain. Saint-Placide is a side street that is right alongside AU BON MARCHÉ, the department store on the Left Bank. Take the *métro* to Saint-Placide and walk toward Au Bon Marché and the Rue des Sèvres. Along the Saint-Placide you'll pass about ten *stock* shops, from the cheap junk type to the designer type.

Best of the bunch is the group owned by LE MOUTON À 5 PATTES which has a children's shop and a designer shop as well as a real-people shop. There were plenty of big-time names (in bins) last time I visited. Names like Gaultier and Ferre, in fact.

Saint-Placide feels a bit seedy and isn't as attractive as Alésia, but there's nothing wrong with the neighborhood, and it is safe. Walk along the street, choosing what interests you; until you come head-on to the Rue de Sèvres, which is a main drag for "real-people" shopping. Because AU BON MARCHÉ is right there, many other retailers have come along with branch stores to catch the overflow department-store traffic. There's a GUERLAIN and a RODIER and a DOROTHÉE BIS and a lot of nice stores. It is not fancy here, but quite serviceable. There is a *métro* in the square (Sèvres-Babylone), or you can take the Rue de Sèvres for one block and hit the really exciting, fancy, expensive stores of the Little Dragons (see page 80).

Suburban

LA DÉFENSE

La Défense is not a neighborhood for tourists, but should be filed in the back of your mind for the time when you swap houses with a French family and move to Paris for a few weeks. La Défense is a high-rise business section in Courbevoie, a suburb of Paris, but along with the businesses there is a huge shopping area with a *hypermarché* (supermarket) and many resources for fun, inexpensive household and life-style items. This is for French yuppies who bring the car and load up on Saturdays. From a sociological perspective, this is modern French shopping—American style!

PALAIS DES CONGRÈS (PORTE MAILLOT)

If you aren't going to La Défense on business, your business may have you a prisoner at the

Palais des Congrès, the big convention center that is best known as the place where the airport bus drops you off. Not scenic, but there are a lot of stores here (over eighty of them)—many are branches of designer shops like CHARLES JOURDAN, LOUIS FÉRAUD, CHRISTIAN DIOR, PIERRE CARDIN, DANIEL HECHTER, ANDRÉ COURRÈGES, etc. Get a Japanese luncheon snack at DAIMARU, a branch of the Tokyo department store. The shopping mall is lacking in ambience but the opportunities to spend are many.

BERCY

You will pass the business suburb of Bercy as you drive to EuroDisney so when you see all those high-rises and the crazy architecture and want to know what's going on, here's the scoop. There's a lot of TV stations here and a lot of business and the big new library and, yes, there's a huge mall. It's not for tourists; do not detour. Keep on keeping on for Mickey Mouse.

MARNE LA VALLÉE/EURODISNEY

So it's not a neighborhood, it's a whole village—you'll never see it, though, if you're headed for EuroDisney. If you've got the kids with you, you'll be hard pressed to not visit Disney (or Dizneigh); you can do it without spending a franc in the park, so take notes.

Take the RER (Regional Express Railway) train—there are about five stations that connect. The one at Opéra is called Auber. You'll have to go down three or four flights of stairs to get to the station. You want Line A4 to Chessy/Marne La Vallée. In 1994 there will be a TGV rail line from Gare de Lyon. Stay tuned. You may also transfer by bus straight from the airport or drive 20 miles east of Paris for the day, the weekend or the week. The easiest by far is the train; the station lets out right before the gates to the park.

Note: Prices on gifts, souvenirs, food and admission tend to be higher than in the U.S. If you just want a souvenir, there are plenty of souvenirs pegged at 25 francs (about $5). Besides, how can you go home with your EuroDisney T-shirt?

Shopping at EuroDisney is divided into several areas: there's stores in the park itself, there's stores in each of the hotels built around the park and then there's this wonderful Festival Disney space with lots of stores and eats that was designed by Frank Gehry and is one of the most interesting parts of the park. Get this: you can go out to the park on the train and wander around and see a lot without ever paying admission to the park! You don't get any rides, of course, but you can see the setup, be impressed by the architecture, wander around the hotels, buy your souvenirs and tell your friends you've seen it.

The stores inside the park sell a combination of Disney, EuroDisney and non-theme merchandise. There is a fair amount of Americana. There is different merchandise in almost every store, with very little crossover so that you can only stand so much after a while anyway. A lot of the merchandise seems recycled from Orlando; you'll find the same items for sale at the Yacht & Beach hotels in Orlando and The Newport Inn in France.

There's an arcade for shopping right at Town Hall and many opportunities to buy souvenirs throughout the park; I'm very happy with the choices at Festival Disney: Disney storybooks in French are a wonderful gift ($5); the Disney characters and titles have been translated into French and make cute postcards. T-shirts range from $15–35. Wallets at $5 and passport cases on strings (to go around the neck) at $7 were my favorite gift items.

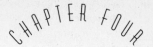
REAL-LIFE RESOURCES

Department Stores

French department stores are for French people; only GALERIES LAFAYETTE and AU PRINTEMPS make a serious attempt to woo American tourists. As a result, Americans know about these two—which are next door to each other and easily hit at once—but aren't very familiar with the other stores. Few Americans even realize that there's a rather large branch of the British icon MARKS & SPENCER across the street from Galeries Lafayette.

The biggies offer a lot of bang for your time but they also sure do get crowded on Saturdays and in summer. If your time in Paris is limited, check out the designer fashions and then all the ready-to-wear clothing floors of a good department store and you will immediately know what's hot and what's not. Spend an hour (maximum, two hours) at Galeries Lafayette's first- and second-floor designer niches for a fast overview of the fashion scene and of what's available. If you have no time to track down the individual shops of your favorite designers, buy at Galeries Lafayette. If you are more interested in tabletop, Au Printemps has an entire housewares store (next door to the mother store) which will give you the big picture in a short period of time.

The truth is that Galeries Lafayette has four different buildings and Au Printemps has another three (this is a total of seven buildings of department store proportions!); there are also scads of street vendors (selling goods from the stores, by the way) and a little alley filled with little stalls between the stores—in short, this place is overwhelming. It's not an easy browse; it won't be fun if you think you are going to tackle it all.

What you need is a plan. I suggest Galeries Lafayette for fashion and Au Printemps Housewares. Then I go to the Galeries Lafayette supermarket (LAFAYETTE GOURMET), MONOPRIX (the dime store); I hit BOUCHARA, the fabric store, and I am outta there. I can do all of this in three hours and have a ball; I suggest you limit your time here and enjoy it. Then go to either the CAFÉ DE LA PAIX or LE GRAND HÔTEL INTERCONTINENTAL for tea. And maybe to American Express for more cash.

AU PRINTEMPS

Most people call it merely Printemps, which means spring. You can walk in feeling like spring and come out hours later like a lion in winter. This store has fabulous print graphics; they do very nice ads in *The New York Times* inviting you to visit them; often they do promotional tie-ins with tour groups and airlines, and even may offer a 10% discount coupon; they have the very nicest fashion show in the rooftop garden. But still they are a very disappointing store to an American who can pick from Saks to Limited Express and who came to Paris for real razzle-dazzle.

About that discount coupon: Mine was in a stack of coupons at the concierge desk at the Meurice—while I got the coupon in the winter season, it was valid for a full year, including the prime time in-season months. You present the card and your passport at the Welcome Service desk in the basement of the main fashion store and you will be given a credit-card-like device that entitles you to a 10% discount. This offer does not apply to food, books or already discounted merchandise. This has nothing to do with the *détaxe*; if you qualify for *détaxe*, you get an additional 13–16% off. (The range depends on what you buy; if it's perfume you'll get 16% discount.)

Created in 1865, Au Printemps is based on the Boulevard Haussmann, but has three other branch stores in Paris. The main store is divided into three separate stores: BRUMMEL, the men's store, which is behind the main store; the Home Store (PRINTEMPS DE LA MAISON) and the fashion store, PRINTEMPS DE LA MODE. For some reason, perfumes are sold in the home store. Not to worry, go right up those escalators.

The best things about Au Printemps are simple:

- excellent design (home fashion) store
- lovely terrace for seeing Paris
- good touristy fashion show (Tuesday all year round at 10 A.M.; also on Friday at 10 A.M. during the high season, March through October and Monday, May through September). Meet under the cupola on the 7th floor of the fashion store (main store).
- nice branch stores all over France (there's an especially nice store in Deauville).

Hours: 9:35 A.M.–7 P.M., Monday through Saturday.

Au Printemps
64 Boulevard Haussmann, 9e (*Métro*: Chaussée-d'Antin)

Printemps Nation
25 Cours de Vincennes, 20e (*Métro*: Porte de Vincennes)

Printemps Italie
30 Avenue d'Italie, 13e (*Métro*: Italie)

Printemps République
10 Place de la République, 11e (*Métro*: République)

BAZAR DE L'HÔTEL DE VILLE (BHV)

If you think that's a funny name for a store, you can call it BHV (pronounced Bay H. Vay in French), or remember that the full name of the store tells you just where it is—directly across from the Hôtel de Ville. The store is famous for its do-it-yourself attitude and for its housewares, and you owe it to yourself to go to the basement (SS) level to see all this stuff. If you are at all interested in gadgets or interior design, you will go nuts. The upper floors are ordinary enough, downstairs can be ordinary—I am not sending you to Paris to buy a lawn mower—but there are little nooks and crannies that will drive you nuts with wonder. I buy the brass lock pieces and string them on necklaces for gifts.

Hours: Monday, Tuesday, Thursday, Friday, and Saturday, 9:30 A.M. to 6:30 P.M.; Wednesday, 9:30 A.M. to 10 P.M.

BAZAR DE L'HÔTEL DE VILLE (BHV)

Rue de Rivoli, 1er (Métro: Hôtel de Ville)

AU BON MARCHÉ

Au Bon Marché is the big department store of the Left Bank. While there are branches of some of the other stores on the Left Bank, this is the one biggie there, and it is convenient to a good bit of your Left Bank shopping. This is the Little Dragons neighborhood, convenient not only to enticing little boutiques, but also to a street of discount stores. (See page 80.)

There are two BHV stores, actually, but the smaller one is devoted to food and entertaining and connects through the basement to the main store...or enter through its own door. The food store is called LA GRANDE ÉPICERIE and it's grand in both size and style. Perfect for gathering your *picnique* ingredients, buying foodstuffs for gifts, getting a snack or just gawking.

Take the escalator upstairs and you'll find a place for a tea or coffee and an indoor flea market! After this portion of the store, you'll find the building next door very traditional and boring. They do have the expected range of first floor cosmetics and accessories, then fashions for the family and even home furnishings and carpets.

Hours: Monday to Saturday, 9:30 A.M. to 6:30 P.M.

Au Bon Marché
Rue de Sèvres, 6e (*Métro*: Sèvres-Babylone)

C&A

This is a Dutch department store famous for its low-end merchandise—rather like Marks & Spencer. You'll find them all over the world. The clothes have more zip to them than the fashions at MARKS & SPENCER; often you can find cute copies of the fad fashions at prices that are appropriate for teens. C&A in Paris is convenient, inexpensive, manageable and even has nice dressing rooms.

Hours: Monday to Saturday, 9:30 A.M. to 7 P.M.

C&A
124 Rue de Rivoli, 1er (*Métro*: Châtelet)
22 Rue du Départ, 14e (*Métro*: Montparnasse)

FRANCK ET FILS

Franck et Fils is actually a specialty store. We're talking refined old lady here. Back behind the elevator, there is a telephone that links up directly to a taxi company. The store is elegant, easy to shop, uncrowded and relatively undiscovered by tourists. There is a branch at the FORUM DES HALLES, but it doesn't compare to the Passy shop. You can find respectable, classical fashions in a well-bought atmosphere geared for Madame. You'll feel very French if you browse, although you may get bored. You are wearing your pearls, aren't you?

Hours: Monday to Saturday, 10 A.M. to 5:30 P.M.

FRANCK ET FILS
80 Rue de Passy, 16e (*Métro*: Muette)

GALERIES LAFAYETTE

Galeries Lafayette loves tourists and very much wants you to spend your money with them. Since about a hundred thousand customers visit this store each day, they obviously have convinced a lot of customers. Whenever I go to Galeries Lafayette I remember the expression "Hell is other people." Well, hell is other people who shop at Galeries Lafayette. Especially in summer. If you are strong, then you deserve to see the three Galeries Lafayette stores: GALFA CLUB (a men's store); the MAIN STORE; and the SPORTS STORE. And don't forget the grocery store (above MONOPRIX).

If the grocery doesn't satisfy for hunger, there also is a snack shop and restaurant called PAVILLON LAFAYETTE (14 Rue de Mogador, 9e), behind the main store. Or there's a *crêpe* stand on the corner—so you won't starve.

Now then, what's good about this zoo?

- The fabulous stained-glass ceiling in the center of the main store and the entire architectural picture—all old-fashioned department stores were created like this, with galleries that ring around a central court. This is one of the few that remain.
- Zillions of designer boutiques—you can get a rather quick look at the fashion scene by these small but edited showcases.
- Huge perfume selection (although Printemps is probably equal and less crowded)—a good way to spritz your way to an asthma attack or a whole new set of friends.
- The kids' department is good, although a lot of the toys are American licenses and expensive; there are versions of all your favorite board games in French (gift idea). From January until Lent there is a small boutique selling carnival costumes, papergoods and treats.

This store also offers a 10% discount coupon; I got mine at the desk of the Meurice. The GL discount card works exactly as described above at AU PRINTEMPS. You may also combine it with your *détaxe* refund—spend 1,200 francs if you are American; 2,800 francs for an EEC passport. GL also has a weekly fashion show, for reservations call 48-74-02-30 or ask your hotel concierge to book.

If you are planning on buying a lot, but it will be a lipstick here, some panty hose there, a blouse on two, and a toy on five, and the thought of writing up all those sales slips on an individual basis makes you nuts, you can use a collector's card. Your purchase is rung up on the cash register, held at the desk, and your card is marked with the amount. You go around shopping all day, clutching your card in your hand. When you are finished, you pay for the grand total. This is one of the easiest ways to get your *détaxe*, since you pay and claim the credit all at once. There's only one problem: After you have paid, you must collect all of your packages. Arrangements may even be made at some stores to ship your purchases directly home. I confess to once being lost on the first floor of Galeries Lafayette and unable to collect my purchase. Yep, I cried.

And in case you think if you've seen one Galeries Lafayette, you've seen them all: there is very little similarity between the store in Paris and the New York version.

Hours: 9:30 A.M. to 6:30 P.M., Monday through Saturday.

GALERIES LAFAYETTE
40 Boulevard Haussmann, 9e (*Métro*: Chaussée-d'Antin)

GALERIES LAFAYETTE CENTRE COMMERCIAL MONTPARNASSE
22 Rue du Départ, 14e (*Métro*: Montparnasse)

MARKS & SPENCER

On Boulevard Haussmann you can zigzag into the Opéra or go immediately into Marks & Spencer. Which would you rather, really? The Marks & Spencer in Paris is amazingly like the main Oxford Street store near Selfridge's in London. Marks & Spencer still is a good place for underwear, for the St. Michael private label brand, and for good, sturdy, inexpensive kids' clothes. But it is a far from elite store, and blue bloods should pass without entering. If you're curious about the most important item, price—well, prices are less in London. However, prices are moderate enough for locals to flock to this resource. There is a food department, not as exciting as the grocery departments in England, but offering British foodstuffs (St. Michael label) nonetheless.

Hours: Monday, Tuesday, Thursday, Friday, and Saturday, 9:30 A.M. to 6:30 P.M.; Wednesday, 10 A.M. to 6:30 P.M.

MARKS & SPENCER

33–45 Boulevard Haussmann, 9e (Métro: Chaussée-d'Antin)

SAMARITAINE

It can be a little confusing to find your way around the separate stores and interconnecting basement, but a this store offers a distinctively French atmosphere. Of the four buildings that make up the store, only one of them is even called Samaritaine. The most important shop is STORE 2, which is behind STORE 4.

The sports department is in STORE 3. Store 4 has records and books and art supplies. But Store 2 is my favorite; it is also the only one with a bathroom. Locals use this resource as we would use Kmart or Target. There is also a roof garden with a great view; you can have some of the benefits of a French department store without going nuts on the Boulevard Haussmann.

Hours: Monday, Wednesday, Thursday, and Saturday, 9:30 A.M. to 7 P.M.; Tuesday and Friday, 9:30 A.M. to 8:30 P.M.

SAMARITAINE

67 Rue de Rivoli, 1er (*Métro*: Châtelet or Pont Neuf)

Shopping Centers

The shopping center of your teen years, like the mall where everyone used to hang out, does not exist in great abundance in Europe. There are a number of malls—many in suburbs like Bercy. In the heart of Paris, there are two important malls (not counting all the *passages* and *galeries*).

FORUM DES HALLES

The Forum des Halles was built to rejuvenate a slum, and serves as an exciting monument to youth, style and shopping. It's a huge square with a courtyard, it's rather American and sterile once you are inside and it's easy to get very lost. Located directly above a *métro* stop and down the street from the YSL discount store, it's conveniently located. It's also a stone's throw from the Beaubourg, so you may want to stop by. If you don't want to, you're really not missing much. There are fast-food joints in the *métro* part of the complex and real restaurants in among the shops in the regular complex. A series of escalators zigzags between the floors; there are master maps throughout the mall to help you find your way. Although a number of designers and upper-priced bridge lines have stores here, the stores are often not as charming as the boutiques on the street can be. The Forum was built in stages; be sure to see the newest part of the mall, which stretches underground.

Most of the stores in the Forum des Halles open between 10 and 10:30 A.M. , close between 7 and 7:30 P.M. on Tuesday through Saturday, and are closed all day Sunday and Monday morning (but open at noon on Monday). All take plastic.

Forum Des Halles
Métro: Châtelet

LES TROIS QUARTIERS

This is what I'd call a mini-mall and it's nothing to write home about, although locals love it and find it very American. Stores here are small (except for the huge perfume/duty free SILVER MOON) and well integrated. I like the mix of designers and upscale suppliers. This is a good way to see a lot of shops in a quick hit without feeling that you're doomed to wander endlessly as you do at the FORUM DES HALLES. Designer shops range from KENZO to CHACOCK; there's a little of everything thrown in. Cathy Nolan goes to the hairdresser here—ALEXANDRE has a branch shop. *Tres chic.*

Les Trois Quartiers
23 Blvd. de la Madeleine, 1er (Métro: Madeleine)

Passages

A *passage* (it rhymes with massage) is a shopping area, exactly like an arcade in London. *Passages* are the equivalent of mini-malls, and are cut into a building's lobby like a throughway. In the early 1800s the buildings were large, often taking up a block. To get from one side to the other at midpoint, a *passage* was built. It is inside the building, so it's totally covered. Doorways lead through the original structure.

There are lots *passages* all over Paris. One of the most famous is the GALERIE VIVIENNE. One doorway is on the Rue Vivienne, the other is on the Rue des Petits-Champs. The *passage* is not surrounded by a greater building, but is directly across from the National Library and near the

Palais-Royal; it has a number of cute shops and the GAULTIER boutique.

The shopowners in a *passage* usually organize themselves, at least informally. Together they will decide if their shops will be open or closed during lunchtime. (The Galerie Vivienne is open during lunchtime.) *Passages* have cheaper rent than regular commercial space, so usually you'll find relatively mundane enterprises (like a printer or bakery) or young designers who are just starting out but may be moving fast.

Métro Shopping

Most of the *métro* stops have little shops in them. These are the kind of shops you find in almost any *métro* or subway—overpriced and not of good quality. The Châtelet station is gigantic (many lines converge here) and so has more of an underground shopping mall built into it than do other stops. You can always buy postcards and souvenirs in these shops. Often street people set up their wares on blankets in the stations. You can bargain here, of course, but watch for fakes. *métro* stop souvenirs are generally inexpensive and make unique gifts.

The Duty Frees

Paris is famous for its duty free shops; this is one of the few cities in the world where there is a lot of duty free style shopping on city streets, not just at the airport. This is because French value added taxes are structured with a special category for luxury goods (perfume is a luxury; eau d'toilette is not). Years ago the government put a very high tax on them. Taxes have been lowered over the years because of unification, and may still go lower on these goods, so the duty free business is changing. But the important thing to understand is that in Paris, all those duty free shops offer a slightly better deal than what you will get at the airport. So don't wait, unless you have to.

Duty-free shops are a good place to buy fragrances and cosmetics, although the price on these items is controlled and may offer you little or no savings from U.S. prices. Concentrate first on French brands, then Italian. On American brands, savings are iffy. This is where homework pays off. Saving $1 on a Lancôme mascara is not my idea of anything to brag about. Sometimes the savings are related to the cost of the dollar. When the dollar was high, I saved $4 on a Lancôme mascara. Now the dollar is lower, and Lancôme prices are higher. Life goes on. But there are enormous savings to be made if you qualify for *détaxe* and shop wisely.

Traditionally a duty-free can give you no more than a 20% discount. You get this discount on one tube of lipstick or on $2,000 worth of merchandise. No more, no less. If, however, you qualify for the *détaxe*, you will get an additional 20% discount. Although one thing has nothing to do with another, duty-frees like to tell you that they give a 40% discount, to make you feel like a lucky duck. To get the 40% discount, *you must qualify for the détaxe*. On the other hand, if you want just a few items and can't begin to think about spending $200 (maybe more), it makes the most sense to shop at a duty-free rather than any other type of makeup store, including a large department store—*except* that if you are saving your department store receipts to qualify for the *détaxe* (see page 49 and 88), you can make a small makeup purchase. You will not get the 20% duty free discount, but you will eventually qualify for the *détaxe* discount. This takes amazing planning; also note that department stores, like airport duty free stores, offer a 13–16% discount, not a 20% discount. This may become standard for all duty frees but is not the policy as we go to press.

Most duty-free shops sell makeup, fragrance and other touristy items, with the service policy of being a one-stop shopping resource. This makes it easier to make the quota for the *détaxe*. So you buy scarves, handbags, combs and other gift items in the free wheeling belief that you are getting a 40% discount on everything. Wrong. Ask what the discount is on each item you are buying. By law, only the luxury items get the big write-off.

If you think this is all nonsense and the complexities of it make you wince (join the club), find a duty free that offers a flat discount to all clients no matter how much you buy. This should be 30%, which is a fair compromise, and it should apply to credit-card purchases. (See page 172.)

Museum Shops

Almost all the Paris museums have gift shops and there are about 50 museums in Paris. Some just sell slides, prints and a few high-minded books. But several are really with it, and their people must have made a trip to the New York Metropolitan Museum of Art to see how it's done. All the fashiony museums have excellent gift shops:

MUSÉE DES ARTS DÉCORATIFS

107 Rue de Rivoli, 1er (*Métro:* Louvre)

It's closed Monday and Tuesday but open on Sunday from 11 A.M. to 5 P.M. The shop and the separate bookstore are wonderful, with crafts items and repro gifts. Prices aren't low but you'll find unique gift items; even a copy of the very first scarf Hermès ever created.

MUSÉE DU LOUVRE

Palais du Louvre, 1er (*Métro:* Louvre)

There's a gift shop under that glass pyramid, and it is a beauty, with two levels of shopping space. The store sells books, postcards and repro gifts. *Beaucoup* fun. You do not have to be admitted into the museum part to shop here, or pay admission. After walking into the pyramid, take the escalator down and you will be in a lobby reminiscent of a train station. Glance around, read a few signs and you'll soon see the gift shop—it's straight ahead.

MUSÉE D'ORSAY

Gare d'Orsay, 7e (Métro: Quai d'Orsay)

The gift shop isn't as wonderful as the architecture, but you can buy prints and some reproductions and a scarf or two. Good selection of postcards.

CENTRE GEORGES POMPIDOU

Centre Georges Pompidou, 4e (Métro: Châtelet)

The gift shop takes up much of the first floor and is a wonderful source for posters, books and postcards. They have the special tubes you need to transport posters so they don't get crushed.

MUSÉE CARNAVALET

29 Rue de Sévigné, 3e (Métro: Saint Paul)

This is one of Marie Jo's favorite museum gift shops. The museum is in the heart of the Marais and documents the history of the city of Paris; the gift shop sells reproductions of antique items— many owned by famous people. I have the Georges Sand stemware. Closed on Mondays.

Souvenir Shops

Paris is loaded with souvenir shops. They congregate around the obvious tourist haunts (Notre Dame, Champs-Élysées, etc.) and line the Rue de Rivoli from Concorde all the way up to the front gate of the Louvre. They all sell more or less the same junk at exactly the same prices. Yes, folks, those prices are nonnegotiable. The only way you can get a break is to deal on the amount you buy. If you buy a few T-shirts, you might get a few francs knocked off. The price of T-shirts fluctuates, by the way, with the dollar: the price in francs varies (note the handwritten signs) so the T-shirts always cost $10. No dummies here. Naturally there are T-shirts which cost more, but you'll have no trouble finding acceptable gifts for $10.

Things to buy at a souvenir stand:

- Toothbrush with your name (a friend's name, you get the idea) in French or some similar name in French.
- Breakfast bowl sponged blue and white, also with name in French.
- Boxer shorts with various Parisian motifs.
- T-shirts with French universities on them.
- Key chains with all kinds of possibilities— miniature Eiffel Towers, street signs, Napoleon, etc.
- Scarves with kitschy tourist-haunt designs that are so bad they are fabulous.

Special-Event Retailing

Paris is filled with special shopping events. Watch for the Braderie de Paris, which is held in December and June at the Porte de Versailles. It's rather like a church bazaar. Speaking French will help but is not required. All the big designers donate items for sale; there are bargains by the ton. Ask your concierge for details and the exact dates, although the event will be advertised in magazines and papers, and we know you read *Madame Figaro* when you are in town, so you probably know it all anyway. There is easy access by *métro*.

HERMÈS has sales twice a year that can only be described as world-class sporting events. Held in March and October, the sales' exact dates are revealed moments before, in ads in the newspapers. Lines begin to form at 7 A.M.; a lucky few are let in when the doors open at 10

A.M. The average wait in line is four hours before admission; items are marked down to just about half price. Lest you gloat too long over the bargain, there is a code worked into your purchase that tells the world your item was bought on sale. It is not obvious, but look for a teeny-tiny S in the scarf, etc.

The thing you really want to catch is the Biennale Internationale des Antiquaires, which is an international antiques fair. We are not talking some small-time international antiques fair with a few dozen chairs and a sofa half-eaten by moths. This is the single biggest, most important antiques event in the world. Usually it is held in September and is at the Grand Palais—which is midpoint between the Place de la Concorde and Rond Point and is most easily reached by a *métro* that puts you right next to it.

The big catch is that the major show is held only every other year. Check in the design trades for the actual dates, ask your decorator or check with your concierge. You need not be a designer to attend.

Annual shows are held at the Grand Palais each year from late November through early December, and they, too, are wonderful. But if you've ever been to the big event, you surely will never forget it.

There are also a number of antiques shows which happen at the same time every year and become special events to plan trips around. April in Paris means only one thing: time for the Brocante de Bastille.

Ask your hotel concierge; look in *Allo Paris* or any of the weekly or monthly guides. The French tourist office can supply you with the dates of these special events and others—antiques shows and special sales, conventions, trade shows and whatnot. Write to the French Government Tourist Office, 610 Fifth Avenue, New York, NY 10020-2493.

Dépôts-Ventes (Resale Shops)

The French pride themselves on being a practical people. They rarely throw anything away, they buy only the best quality and use it forever, they hate waste of any sort. But if someone in the family dies, or if someone should fall on hard times, he can sell his fine possessions at a *dépôts-vente*. Or, knowing that good merchandise is being sold, he will frequent a *dépôts-vente*. No one in Paris is ever ashamed to be seen buying used items. They think it's smart. I do too. Following are some of the most famous *dépôts-ventes*.

RÉCIPROQUE

These are actually three separate shops in a row. The main Réciproque shop has two floors, so don't forget to go downstairs. There are racks and racks of clothes, all clean—you'll find separates, shoes, evening clothes and complete ensembles. You must look through carefully and know your merchandise, although the labels always are in the clothes. Not everything is used, or seriously used—many designers sell samples or photography items. Every big name is represented here; this is the best single resource for used couture clothing. A Chanel suit will cost near $2,000, so prices are not dirt cheap.

In the gift shop you'll find silver, tablecloths and china. This is obviously a hit-or-miss operation, but give it a look-see. You also can buy used sports equipment, children's clothes, men's clothing and accessories in their own shop at No. 123. Designer handbags at $50–$100 are the best deal in town.

RÉCIPROQUE

95, 101, and 123 Rue de la Pompe, 16e (*Métro*: Pompe)

CATHERINE BARIL

Another contender in the used-designer-clothing wars, Baril has two shops with top-drawer stuff—YSL, Chanel, the works. There is also some new clothing—samples and the like. The shop is closed Monday morning (hours are 2 P.M. to 7 P.M.), but opens at 10 A.M. Tuesday to Saturday.

CATHERINE BARIL

14 and 25 Rue de la Tour, 16e (Métro: Trocadéro)

DIDIER LUDOT

This shop is not easy to find, so have patience and remember that it is on the gallery side of the building, not the street side. It is a very tiny shop run by a man who really cares about the clothes and their history, and he tries to sell only top-of-the-line used designer goods, specializing in Hermès, Céline and Chanel. You may find old Hermès bags from the 1930s here. The entire gallery is fun, but this store is a standout for old-clothes junkies. Prices are high for quality items. The easiest way to get there is to find yourself at the Comédie Français outside the Palais-Royal *métro* station. Zig to the right into the open arcade then hug the left where the arcade is covered. Shops line the walkway. Ludot is here.

DIDIER LUDOT

24 Passage de la Galerie Montpensier, near Palais-Royal, 1er (Métro: Palais-Royal)

Bargain Basements

ANNA LOWE

Since the front of Anna Lowe has her name on the door and then the words *haute couture*, you might think we've made a mistake sending you to such a fancy place. Trust us. Despite the beige marble and the fine windows, Anna Lowe's prices are good for designs by major names. Prices are not cheap, but these aren't cheap clothes. They will cost at least 25% less than in the Paris shops. This is the kind of shop Mother would call "a good find." They take plastic and speak English. Some of the clothes are models' samples; if you're size 6 or 8 you will do very well here. Hours: Monday to Friday, 10 A.M. to 7 P.M.; Saturday hours: 3 P.M. to 7 P.M. This shop is right off the faubourg-Saint-Honoré; don't miss it.

ANNA LOWE

35 Avenue Matignon, 8ᵉ (Métro: Franklin D. Roosevelt)

BABS

The beige carpet and fancy surroundings make it seem unbelievable that this is a bargain basement. The help is not really friendly if you are just browsing, but once you show them you are a serious shopper, things warm up. There always has been an incredible selection of daytime dresses, separates and evening wear. Most labels are cut out. But it's a lot fancier here than at Loehmann's.

BABS

29 Avenue Marceau, 16ᵉ (Métro: Alma Marceau)

BETTY

After BABS, it's a long way to Betty—on the *métro* and emotionally. The bad news about Betty: It's a long way to go when it could be a wasted trip. The good news about Betty: The shop is across from the *marché* at Place d'Aligre, which is one of the most colorful *marchés* in Paris and is worth visiting; while you're there you can stick your head into Betty and check it out. Betty seems to specialize in very ordinary women's suits for business and yardgoods and some clothes from couture house Léonard. For $250 you could own a current, silk-knit Léonard dress that is certainly the bargain of the century. You can make a sarong skirt with the Léonard fabric and very little sewing ability. Check for defects in printing on those tricky Léonard prints.

Hours: Tuesday, Wednesday, and Friday, 8:30

A.M. to 12:30 P.M.; Thursday and Saturday, 8:30 A.M. to 12:30 P.M. and 2:30 P.M. to 4:30 P.M.

BETTY

10 Place d'Aligre, 12e (*Métro*: Ledru-Rollin)

BERNARD MARIONNAUD

While it is on Avenue Victor Hugo, do not think it's on the Avenue Victor Hugo near the Étoile. This Victor Hugo is in Clamart, which is about five minutes outside of Paris past the Porte de Versailles and is a working-class neighborhood. There are three other outlets of this shop, but they aren't convenient and they don't begin to compare. If you are ready for one of the shopping adventures of your life, make the trek out to Clamart.

Note: Do not do this if you only have three, four or maybe five days in Paris. Your time is too precious to travel all the way out here.

Bernard Marionnaud is famous in French retailing and perfume circles for creating the discount perfume business. He sells more than fragrance in Clamart, but he is primarily a resource for cosmetics and fragrances. Before I go into rhapsodic rantings and ravings about this store, a warning: You will not get any better price on cosmetics or fragrance here than in Paris. In fact, you may not get the very lowest price on the non-cosmetics items, either—but you will get a good low price and will have a great time. What Clamart offers is selection. I have never seen such a selection, especially at a discount resource. Clamart offers three types of merchandise—regular drugstore sundries (hairspray, curlers, pantyhose), designer accessories (S. T. Dupont, Cartier, Balenciaga), and the full line of the world's most famous cosmetics and fragrance companies. Not only do they have every size of perfume and toilet water, but they also have all the promotional gifts—those tote bags filled with sunscreen, the men's dop kit with grooming aids, etc. They even carry Guerlain, which is rather extraordinary, since Guerlain is rarely, if ever, sold outside of Guerlain shops and is never, never discounted.

This store takes credit cards and the staff is extremely friendly. If you don't want to spring for a taxi for the considerable distance, take the *métro* to Porte de Versailles and get a taxi there. Remember that you may not save back your taxi fares, but you will have the time of your life.

Hours: Sunday, 9:30 A.M. to 1 P.M.; Monday, 2 P.M. to 8 P.M.; Tuesday to Saturday, 8:30 A.M. to 8 P.M.

BERNARD MARIONNAUD

91 Avenue Victor Hugo, Clamart, 16e (*Métro:* Porte de Versailles, then taxi)

CHIFF-TIR

Chiff-Tir is not one of the great finds of the Western world—but you probably will walk right by it anyway, so you can decide rather easily if it's your cup of tea. Chiff-Tir is an outlet for linens and tableware. Most French people shop here, especially for their kids' sheets—they have a wide selection of sheets with popular cartoon characters. The sheets happen to be much cheaper than in the United States. If you have a good eye and don't mind looking through some very average merchandise, you can find some nice gifts—or personal items at extremely inexpensive prices. If you entertain outdoors, or have kids, and like your tables to look divine without going the Souleiado-Porthault-Pratesi route, Chiff-Tir may solve your problems. There are many branches of this firm but the one you will walk right by is right off the Place Madeleine and across the street from the new mini-mall, LES TROIS QUARTIERS.

CHIFF-TIR

1 Rue Duphot, 1er (*Métro:* Madeleine)
134 Rue de Rivoli, 1er (*Métro:* Louvre)
56 Rue de Seine, 6e (*Métro:* Odéon)

L'ANNEXE DES CRÉATEURS

The shop is crowded, and lacks charm, but is crammed with clothes and bolts of fabric—if you like this kind of thing, *voilà*. They have sizes up to 44, which is an American size 12. You won't have to make a special trip; the location is close to many places in every woman's journey through Paris, so it's no trouble to get there—it's half way between Madeleine and the big department stores on Boulevard Haussmann. Stop in to check out hats, accessories, mens clothing; the good stuff begins at $100.

L'ANNEXE DES CRÉATEURS

19 Rue Godot-de-Mauroy, 9ᵉ (Métro: Madeleine)

MENDÈS

Mendès is a jobber who now owns the rights to Yves Saint-Laurent's Rive Gauche. The shop is devoted to various YSL lines—Variations and the lesser lines are sold downstairs; the good stuff is upstairs. Possibly the new Merloz line will be sold here too.

It's very hard to characterize this shop as the quality and selection of goods varies. Certainly don't buy from the Variations line just because it's YSL and you can finally afford to buy YSL. Make sure you've really got a winner. There are a number of classics sold from the racks here—you can see their deriviation from the Rive Gauche line and note the less expensive fabrications. But some of the stuff sold in this part of Mendès is, well, junky.

Upstairs is another story—this is the *crème de la crème*. The *crème* just happens to be old. Possibly very old. There are ball gowns, sportswear separates, blouses and some accessories and even velvet bustiers. Sizes vary dramatically.

Just because this shop is on Rue Montmartre, do not think it is in the famous section of Paris called Montmartre. It's not. It is about three blocks from the FORUM DES HALLES; just stay on the Rue Montmartre until you get there. The numbers should go down if you're going in the right direction. If you end up on the Rue du faubourg Montmartre, you went the wrong way. The store looks like an office building from out front with smoky glass doors; there is a small sign. If you feel lost, ask in any of the jobbers nearby. They all know Mendès.

Hours: Monday to Thursday, 9:30 A.M. to 6:30 P.M.; Friday, 9:30 A.M. to 5 P.M.; Saturday, 9:30 A.M. to 4:30 P.M.

MENDÈS

65 Rue Montmartre, 2ᵉ (*Métro*: Les Halles)

TANGARA

This is a private shoppers club which anyone may join. In fact, after you join, you'll get mail from Paris that will warm your heart. The location is not in the regular tourist stream of things, but they are open on Sunday, so you can make time then. Tangara sells major big time names for men and women, as well as shoes and handbags. I bought a Charles Jourdan summer bag for $100 that I still use. Prices are 40% off French retail; there are end-of-season sales and promotions. If you are not a member, you must go with someone who is a member or join up at the door. Membership was free when I signed up. You get an orange and white plastic membership card to present when you enter thereafter. Note that the clothes are expensive designer models so that while prices are less than retail, they are still stiff.

TANGARA

92 Quai de Jemmapes, 10ᵉ (*Métro*: République)

MI-PRIX

This store is far from fancy. It's not even convenient for most visitors to Paris. But the bargains? Worth the trip. Mi-Prix has a very weird combination of items—the junkiest of no-name merchandise, some very nice skiwear, a fabulous collection of Maud Frizon and Walter Steiger shoes (and boots), Bottega Veneta close-outs, Philippe Model hats—and almost giveaway prices. The store is packed with merchandise; much is current. The shoes could be as current as last season or as old as your grandmother. But Maud Frizon styles are so offbeat that an old pair of shoes can look perfect many years later. And everything is brand new. This is where I got a pair of Bottega Veneta, black, woven leather ballet slippers for $50.

If you are attending a trade show at the Porte de Versailles, this is a must. Also check the newspapers for ads for *brocante* and antiques shows which may be held in this area, so you can combine agendas. It's hard to convince yourself to come all the way out here for one store, when it is a matter of hit or miss, but I've never been sorry I did it. Walk from the convention center along Boulevard Victor about two blocks; there are some other shops and discounters as well.

MI-PRIX
27 Boulevard Victor, 15e (*Métro:* Porte de Versailles)

TEXAFFAIRES
Conveniently located near the Hôtel de Ville, Texaffaires is the outlet for Descamps sheets, towels and robes. The colors are beautiful, the stock is huge, and the light pours through the large windows and makes you want to buy everything in sight; everything in those yummy Descamps colors, anyway. A child's bathrobe is $25; a man's, $50. There's more merchandise downstairs. This is not current stuff, but a terry robe of high quality is a classic—so who cares? Texaffaires is closed Sunday; they open at 10:30 A.M.

TEXAFFAIRES
7 Rue de Temple, 3e (*Métro:* Hôtel de Ville)

STOCK BIDERMANN

Located in the République discount area, Bidermann is the kind of place where you may buy a quality man's suit at a quality price. Men who always have wanted an Yves Saint-Laurent but couldn't afford it may be impressed—and lucky. A true find; many other big names as well. Yes, Bidermann is Regine's brother. Please note that these suits are made for European men; big American bodies may take a different size or find the jackets are snug under the arms. Try it on, sir. Good news: they open at 8:30 A.M.; bad news, they are closed from 12 P.M.–2 P.M.

STOCK BIDERMANN
 114 Rue de Turenne, 3ᵉ (*Métro*: Saint Paul)

Street Merchants

Paris street merchants come in two categories: imitation and real. Most of the merchants around the department stores—the ones with the carts who seem to be selling such great bargains—work for the department stores. Prices are fixed—not negotiable.

The guys in front of Saint-Germain-des-Prés are more authentic street merchants—although many of them have been there selling the same stuff for years. But still, it has its charm.

If you are expecting to find *faux* Chanel or Louis Vuitton on the streets, as you do in New York, forget it. The French have very strict laws about fake merchandise and it's certainly NOT out on the streets.

Tag Sales and Fairs

The French do not know from tag sales. But they do have weekly neighborhood markets that have a *brocante* day. B*rocante* is used junk that would never really be called antique. It is the same kind of item you see at a tag sale. If this sort of thing interests you, find the market day and take a look.

There are more *brocante* dealers at the big markets. Big flea markets are licensed by the city of Paris. Each stall owner pays taxes to the city for his stall and the right to be there. But on the fringes of each market are the illegal guys. Traditionally they are not dealers, but people with leftovers who are selling exactly what you would see at a tag sale.

For a list of *brocante* fairs, see page 209.

Antique Clothes

Antique clothes or used clothes are called *fripes* in French, and are a big item. You can buy them at markets or from dealers. Almost every *marché* has a few *brocante* dealers who sell old pillowcases and camisoles. Clothes from the 1950s and '60s are hot as are all American looks, especially western, southwestern, cowboy and rock and roll. I found a dealer who specializes in hats from the 1950s and '60s. Designer labels are hard to come by and quite dear.

Rentals

About Madame's ball gown. The proper place to rent a couture gown is SOMMIER, 3 Passage Brady, 10ᵉ. The French, being a very practical people, believe in the rental business; therefore, it works. Since French women want only the finest quality and are too practical to buy a couture gown for a once-in-a-lifetime formal event, they rent. If it's been your dream to wear a couture gown, you can have a very good choice at about $100 for the night.

French Factory Outlets

Yes, the French have factory outlets right there in Paris. But no, they probably aren't worth your time, energy or money. Resale shops are fabulous in Paris; if you want a good break on quality merchandise, use them. Factory outlets are for French locals. If you're living in France, or have a car and are merely curious, give them a whirl.

Paris Nord

This is the kind of place that sounds great if a French person tells you about it or you happen to read a write-up in a book or magazine. It sounds like everything you know and love—seventy-two shops selling at factory prices, designer goods, overruns, etc.

The name of the village is the Commercial Center de Paris Nord/Ursine Center. It's about a half-hour drive from Paris, is close to Charles de Gaulle International Airport, and is open from 10 A.M. to 8 P.M. Wednesday through Sunday.

This is a very suburban center. To a tourist, it seems to be located in the middle of nowhere. (It is in the middle of nowhere.)

While there certainly are a ton of stores here, and they are in the factory-outlet tradition, most of the names and labels mean little to us. For the most part they are low-end or moderately-priced goods. Designer things are the exception, not the rule, although designer shops are slowly gaining ground.

The prices, as at all factory outlets, may not be so cheap. The merchandise also may be out of style or very old.

Commercial Center–X%

X% is the name of the center, honest. It's at Ile St. Denis and is open Wednesday through Sunday from 10 A.M. to 8 P.M.

This is not a great neighborhood. The designers are not big-name, but the quality is better than it is at Paris Nord.

Stock Markets

The word for factory overruns in French is *stock*, and so you will find that most factory stores have the word *stock* in their name. These goods are almost always discounted. In a few cases, the word *soldes* comes after the designer's name, and this means the sale merchandise is sold there. In this text we have several sections for bargain basements and *stock* shops and also list the *stock* or sale shop at the main listing of a more famous designer or establishment.

To Market, to Market

One of the difficulties of shopping in Paris is deciding which markets to visit and which to pass up. Unlike most other cities that usually have one or two good markets, Paris is crawling with them. There are actually dozens of them, and it's impossible to get to them all unless you spend a month doing little else.

Most food markets are closed on Monday mornings; anything that is more or less daily which is open on a Sunday is not open on a Monday. The Rue de Buci gets a slow start on Mondays but the action builds. Most flea markets are Saturday and Sunday events although local markets may have *brocante* on Friday and the big flea market at Saint Ouen is open on Monday as well as weekends.

Remember:

- Dress simply; the richer you look, the higher the price. If you wear an engagement ring, or have one of those wedding bands that spells RICH AMERICAN in *pavé* diamonds, leave it in the hotel safe. I like to wear blue jeans and to try to fit in with the crowd; I also have a pair of French eyeglasses to complete my costume.

- Check with your hotel concierge about the neighborhood where the market is located. It may not be considered safe for a woman to go there alone, or after dark. I don't want to be paranoid, but crime in market areas can be higher than in tourist areas—especially outdoor markets. I had a terrible fright at Saint Ouen just last year; it could have been worse. Watch out.

- Have a lot of change with you. It's difficult to bargain and then offer a large bill and ask for change. As a bargaining point, be able to say you only have so much cash on hand.

- If you look like a tourist, the price may start out higher; if you don't know much about what you are buying, the price also may start higher. You do not need to speak any specific language, however, to make a good deal. Bargaining is an international language of emotion, hand signs, facial expressions, etc. If you feel you are being taken, walk away.

- Branded merchandise sold on the street can be hot or counterfeit.

- Go early if you expect the best selection. Go late if you want to make the best deals.

- Never trust anyone (except a qualified shipping agent) to mail anything for you.

- Make sure you are buying something you can legally bring back to the States; don't buy tortoiseshell boxes or combs, because those beauties will be impounded by U.S. Customs. Antique ivory requires the proper paperwork.

- Don't pay the asking price on *brocante* (used junk) unless you want to give the vendor the privilege of telling all his friends what a chump you are. You may find very little room to bargain on more serious items. If you speak perfect French, you may have an edge. You may encounter a bit of anti-American sentiment, usually expressed by an unwillingness to bargain and a shrug of the shoulders.

In Paris, many market areas are so famous that they have no specific street address. Usually it's enough to name the market to a cabbie, but ask your concierge if you need more in the way of directions. Buses usually service market areas; the *métro* goes everywhere and usually is the best bet.

Big Markets of Paris

Sunday is the big day for flea markets, but Vanves is considered best on a Saturday. Food markets alternate in various neighborhoods, you can find a good one any day of the week. There is a food market on Sunday one block over from the Vanves flea market.

RUE DE BUCI

The Rue de Buci is behind the church of Saint-Germain-des-Prés. This is a flower and food market that is colorful and quaint and warm and postcard-picturesque. Although this is a big antiques shop neighborhood, the market does not sell *brocante*. If you only go to one street market in Paris, if you are looking for one food market, one perfect French experience, one picnic-to-go—this is it. This is everyone's fantasy of Paris. There are vendors on both the Rue de Seine and the Rue de

Buci: there's fresh fruits and vegetables piled high on tables, buckets and buckets of brightly-colored flowers, rotisserie chickens, even seashells and sponges. There are a few grocery stores and take-out food joints as well. Come hungry; leave very satisfied. Avoid Monday mornings if possible. (*Métro*: Saint-Germain-des-Prés)

PLACE D'ALIGRE

The Place d'Aligre has a covered indoor market (for butchers, etc.), an open flower and vegetable market, several tables devoted to *brocante* dealers and even a few shops along the way. BETTY, a good discount source, is right here. The *brocante* is very much of tag-sale quality, and you may be annoyed that you came so far if you were searching for the jewel of the Nile. This market is open every day except Monday but closes at about 1 P.M. While ready-to-wear is sold here, it is exactly what Grandma Jessie would call *dreck*, if you'll pardon her French. The yard goods are worthy buys from nearby factories. This market has a real-people Paris feel to it that will make you feel like an insider. (*Métro*: Ledru-Rollin or Gare de Lyon)

PUCES DE VANVES

This market is not like any other market; it's more like a bunch of neighbors who all went in together for one of those big five-family garage sales. The garage sale just happens to stretch for a mile or so. The market is L-shaped: On the main part of the street are the licensed vendors who pay taxes to the city; on the branch part are the illegal, tag-sale vendors—who are the most fun. The tag-sale people's goods are of lesser quality than those of the pros, but together they make for wonderful strolling and browsing. If you don't have much time or can't stand the strain of Saint-Ouen, this is a neighborhood affair that is perfect for a Sunday—although it is also open on Saturday. Early birds get the worms, of course. Saturday is considered the right day to shop Vanves.

The main part of the market is on the Avenue Georges-Lafenestre. With the legal and the illegal guys, there are almost two hundred vendors here. Prices are the best in town: I bought a plaster virgin for 10 FF; an old postcard album (empty) for 50 FF and numerous *fèves*, all for 10 FF each. I splurged on a green glass necklace from the 1960s at 150 FF. There's a *crêpe* stand at the bend in the road; the street market on Sunday enhances the experience. Start early: 9 A.M. is late for Saturday, but just right for Sunday. (*Métro:* Porte de Vanves)

PUCES DE MONTREUIL

Real people of the world, unite, sing "La Marseilles," and run out to the *marché* of Montreuil. This immense market has absorbed three other nearby markets and that has a huge path of illegal vendors that stretches from the *métro* all the way across a bridge to the beginning of the market proper; this is a junk fair with a few diamonds so artfully hidden that you may throw up your hands in disgust.

There's a good selection of *fripes* (used clothes), Victorian bed linens, old hats, new perfumes (look, Mom, who needs *détaxe*?), work clothes, cheap clothes, records, dishes, junk, junk and more junk. Did I mention there is a lot of junk? This is a really low-end market without any charm whatsoever. Dealers work this market very thoroughly—it runs a good 10% to 20% cheaper than Saint-Ouen. But it is 50% harder to find anything good. This is for those with a strong heart and a good eye; princesses and blue bloods need not apply. (*Métro:* Porte de Montreuil)

MARCHÉ AUX PUCES

This is the famous one; the one you are thinking of if you think Paris only has one flea market. See my section on the markets of Saint-Ouen on page 210 for the lowdown. (*Métro:* Porte de Clignancourt)

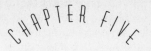

CHAPTER FIVE

PARIS À LA MODE

The French Couture

Couture is considered the epitome of French style. It also has become the international statement of fashion and elegance. *Haute couture* translates as fancy seams, and when you're talking about couture and realize that you are talking about $30,000 garments, you'd better believe that you get very fancy seams.

French couture actually was begun by an Englishman, Charles Frederick Worth, who designed for the Empress Eugénie and created his own distinctive look—flounced skirts balanced by crinolines. (The House of Worth still is known today for its fragrance division, by the way.) Worth worked in the mid- to late-1800s; a new set of couturiers sprang to fame in the turn-of-the-century high-fashion years that ended with World War I. The War to End All Wars also ended a certain life-style forever, and gave much more freedom to women —their garments reflected their change of status, and couturiers such as Paul Poiret and Madeleine Vionnet sprang into vogue for their outlandish designs that had the chutzpah to show off a woman's body.

Christian Dior sparked the world of couture in 1947, right after World War II, with his New Look, and couture has continued to evolve since then as a combination of high style and high inspiration that influenced all other levels of ready-to-wear. Copies of couture designs were absorbed into American culture (the Lord & Taylor couture buyer even had to bring her clothes out of Paris through enemy lines during World War I) and made up American fashion until the early 1950s, when the first American designers of ready-to-wear began to emerge. Dior's assistant, Yves Saint-Laurent, emerged as the *Wunderkind* of couture in 1959, and a group of Young Turks who today hold the silken threads emerged as the powers that be during this time.

Yet surprisingly the couture is not made up just of the names you have come to recognize— from the older, well-established names such as Christian Dior and Hubert de Givenchy to the younger names such as Emanuel Ungaro and Yves Saint-Laurent. There are many couturiers you have never heard of—they are registered with the Chambre Syndicale de la Couture Parisienne (founded in 1868, my dear) and must meet stringent requirements to be couturiers. They too show and do custom work, and every now and then they get discovered by the press and made into stars. In order to encourage more young people to cut in line, the Chambre has even loosened up the rules a tad and tried to ease the cost of showing. Among the new thoughts: you can show the collection on video; you just have to have 75 outfits.

This hasn't helped enormously, Paris still shrugs its shoulders and twice a year asks itself what purpose is served by presenting couture collections. Some houses choose to skip a season or not show at all. No one seems to mind.

Occasionally the head of a house never actually gets the Chambre's approval, so that technically they are not members—such as the House of Balenciaga or Chanel—but when you have that kind of talent, no one seems to remember or care if you are registered.

Usually the designer owns the house that bears his name, although in these days of buyouts and takeovers, it is not unusual for a corporation to buy a design firm. Karl Lagerfeld designs for several houses, conglomerates and big firms and does very nicely on salary and royalties.

A designer makes his name but not his fortune in couture. (He makes his fortune in perfume, in case you're wondering.) It costs well over $3 million to mount a couture collection these days; the cost of the clothes does not compensate for the cost of producing them. Yves Saint-Laurent considers his couture collection a gift to his customers. Indeed, even at $10,000 for a dress or $20,000 to $40,000 for a suit or gown, the prices are possibly not so outrageous—considering the man-hours and labor-intensive care that go into this kind of dressmaking.

Who pays that kind of money for a garment? Only a handful of women; there are thought to be fewer than 2,500 couture customers left in the world. Designers often list the number of regular couture customers they can count. Dior claims about 500 customers; Saint-Laurent, some 750. Nonetheless, the opening of a collection is a big event to society ladies, buyers, designers and the press. While couture showings are held over a period of months and anyone can attend them free, the cachet is in attending the opening, which actually is a press opening.

This event is free to press and Ladies (that's with a capital L) who get invitations, but costs a *caution* to buyers, which is a fee ranging from $300 to $5,000 per house. The *caution* may be a minimum purchase. The cost of a garment varies and most garments have three prices—the price to a buyer (the steepest); the regular price (about 30% less expensive than the buyer's price); and the sample price, which is the price for the garment shown on the runway and not bespoke, as all other couture garments are. Some buyers pay for the rights to copy the garments they buy; some buy *tissus*, which are actual patterns to a style. Pattern companies choose certain *tissus* and pay for them and then provide a royalty on the pattern. (The Vogue Pattern Company always has provided couture designs to the American sewing public.)

The customer who attends an opening is provided with a pad, a pencil and a list of the garments to be shown that is much like a menu. Each garment is numbered. The patron either marks the menu by putting an *x* on the style number or marks her pad with the styles she is serious about. Later she will return to the salon and work privately with her own saleswoman or *vendeuse*, who will show her the garments she is interested in. After the selection has been made, Madame will be measured thoroughly. If she is a new customer (Where has Madame been?), a dummy must be built to her exact measurements. If she is a repeat customer, her new measurements will be compared to those of her existing mannequin. There will be three fittings several weeks apart. Every aspect of the garment will be made to measure by hand with exacting care.

You need not be a couture customer to see a collection (thank God). After the big brouhaha at the time of the opening has died down, you are welcome to visit the salon and see the show. However, in these days of austerity, a house no longer has live models for as long a showing period as in the old days. Don't be surprised if you are shown a videotape. You can call a house directly and reserve a seat (seats must be reserved; drop-ins are frowned upon), or ask your hotel concierge to do so. Most tourists rely on the concierge route; you'll show more individual style if you do it yourself. All houses have English-speaking help.

Do not show up in your London Fog raincoat with your camera in hand. If you have a garment made by the designer, it is a nice touch to wear it. You need not. Remember that you will be treated according to how well-dressed you are. If possible, arrange to attend the show with someone who buys—you will then be treated with more warmth, and possibly a little respect. Serious customers are known throughout the small world of couture; new customers are introduced to the refined inner workings of the system by their refined (and rich) friends.

You can go to a couture show without the obligation to buy, and you needn't feel shabby just because you haven't got the latest little creation by Karl Lagerfeld dripping from your padded shoulders. Have your self-confidence fully in place. You will not fool the *vendeuse* when you walk into a couture showroom—her trained eye will size up your pocketbook (inside and out) in a matter of seconds. Try for an honest approach like, "I've heard that the couturiers sell their samples at the end of the season. Will you be selling samples here?" Do not ask:

"What size are the samples?" (8)

"Can I afford them?" (If you have to ask...)

"Do you take plastic?" (*Mais oui*)

A few tips for *les américaines* who make it to the early shows:

- Yes, you can wear a hat and gloves and your fur and all your jewelry.
- Press shows may or may not be held in the couture house—sometimes they are held in hotels or museums, or even the park.
- The lights will stay on during the show—all the better to see you, my dear.
- French audiences are very verbal and appreciative if they like something—you clap for each number you like and make no noise at all for the ones you hate. If the outfit is a bomb, it's pretty easy to tell by this method. Stand when the collection is over and give the designer an ovation when he parades down the runway (which he will do only for the first two or three shows).

Naturally, the big trick is to get to an early show. To pull this off, you need to make the phone call yourself (the concierge can't do it for you) and be assertive and demanding without being too bossy or too *américaine*. You say something like, "I am in town from New York for just a few days and need to come in for the show tomorrow. I buy only Scherrer, you know." Or, "I AM coming tomorrow. What time is the opening? Please reserve me a seat." Make sure you mention that you plan to buy; no browsers at the big time. Some houses have just a few days of big shows and then show the line in private thereafter. This is no fun. Some houses have ten days of shows; after the first two or three days it is relatively easy to get in.

- Get there early for a good seat. Press shows have reserved seats (with celebs in the front rows and a distinct ranking by money and press power thereafter).
- Dress well.
- Don't forget to applaud.

If you have your eye on an outfit and happen to be the correct sample size (8), often you can buy the sample right after the show. You cannot take it home with you until the house is finished using it, but you can pay for it and consider it yours. When you come back for your private appointment after the show, ask your *vendeuse* to "put a hold" on the garment you fancy. When the garment is no longer needed for shows, it will be spruced up and altered for you—if need be. The house will ship and insure for you; you will get *détaxe*. No one will ever know you have bought a sample. You can also order shoes and accessories this way, but you must be the size that the model wore. All items will be 50% less than the regular individual price. We still are talking about more than $100!

BALMAIN, 44 Rue François-1er, 8e. Tel.: 47-20-35-34.

PIERRE CARDIN, 27 Avenue de Marigny, 8e. Tel.: 42-66-92-25.

CARVEN, 6 Rond Point des Champs-Élysées, 8e. Tel.: 43-59-17-52.

CHANEL, 31 Rue Cambon, 1er. Tel.: 42-61-54-55.

ANDRÉ COURRÈGES, 40 Rue François-1er, 8e. Tel.: 47-20-70-44.

CHRISTIAN DIOR, 30 Avenue Montaigne, 8e. Tel.: 47-23-54-44.

LOUIS FÉRAUD, 88 Rue du faubourg-Saint-Honoré, 8e. Tel.: 42-66-44-60, 42-65-27-29.

GIVENCHY, 3–6–8 Avenue George V, 8e. Tel.: 47-23-81-36.

GRES, 1 Rue de la Paix, 2e. Tel.: 42-61-58-15.

HERMÈS, 24 Rue du faubourg-Saint-Honoré, 8e. Tel.: 42-65-21-68.

CHRISTIAN LACROIX, 73 Rue du faubourg-Saint-Honoré, 8e. Tel.: 42-65-79-08.

LANVIN, 15–22 Rue du faubourg-Saint-Honoré, 8e. Tel.: 42-65-14-40.

REVILLON, 40 Rue La Boétie, 8e. Tel.: 45-61-98-98.

NINA RICCI, 17 Avenue Montaigne, 8e. Tel.: 47-23-78-88.

YVES SAINT-LAURENT, 5 Avenue Marceau, 16e. Tel.: 47-23-72-71.

SIDONIE LARIZZI, 8 Rue Marignan, 8e. Tel.: 43-59-38-87.

TORRENTE, 9 Rue du faubourg-Saint-Honoré, 8e. Tel.: 42-23-61-94.

EMANUEL UNGARO, 2 Avenue Montaigne, 8e. Tel.: 47-23-61-94.

GUY LAROCHE, 29 Avenue Montaigne, 8e. Tel.: 47-23-78-72, 47-47-15-00.

HANAE MORI, 17–19 Avenue Montaigne, 8e. Tel.: 47-23-52-03.

PACO RABANNE, 7 Rue du Cherche-Midi, 6e. Tel.: 42-22-87-80.

JEAN-LOUIS SCHERRER, 51 Avenue Montaigne, 8^e. Tel.: 43-59-55-39.

JEAN PATOU, 7 Rue Saint-Florentin, 8^e. Tel.: 42-60-36-10.

French Big Names

AZZEDINE ALAÏA

Tunisian-born Alaïa shocked Paris fashion with his skintight high-fashion clothes and his first boutique in the then up-and-coming Marais neighborhood. Now people expect the unusual from him; get a look at the architecture of this place and you know he'll never disappoint. The clothes are only for the young, or those with figures like movie stars, but the man is on the cutting edge of fashion and retail. Like many shops in the Marais, this one opens at 11 A.M.

AZZEDINE ALAÏA

7 Rue de Moussy, 4e (*Métro*: Saint Paul)

ALAÏA STOCK

60 Rue de Bellechasse, 7e (*Métro*: Solférino)

AGNÈS B.

An international chain of ready-to-wear shops selling casual clothes with enough of a fashion look for make them appropriate for big city wearing. Jazzier than the Ann Taylor look, but not too jazzy. These two stores next door to each other right down the road from the FORUM DES HALLES gives you both the regular line and the younger looks.

AGNÈS B.

3 and 6 Rue de Jour, 1er (*Métro*: Etienne-Marcel)

CACHAREL

Jean Cacharel made his name in America when he introduced charming clothes in precious prints. Thankfully he has graduated from sweet along with the rest of us, and now does a wide line of separates that are moderately priced. I prefer Cacharel for children's clothes rather than for adult fashion; there is a discount shop that sells the whole shebang.

CACHAREL
    34 Rue Tronchet, 8ᵉ (*Métro:* Madeleine)
    5 Place des Victoires, 1ᵉʳ (*Métro:* Bourse)

CACHAREL STOCK
    114 Rue d'Alésia, 14ᵉ (*Métro:* Alésia)

PIERRE CARDIN

Pierre Cardin has so many shops in Paris, owns so many fabulous outlets for his creativity (including Maxim's) and licenses so many goods that it's impossible to tell you where to shop for his things. There is the main boutique on the Rue du faubourg-Saint-Honoré to get you started. Another shop on Victor Hugo. And the beat goes on.

PIERRE CARDIN
    27 Avenue Victor Hugo, 16ᵉ (*Métro:* Victor Hugo)

PIERRE CARDIN PRESTIGE
    29 Rue du faubourg-Saint-Honoré, 8ᵉ (*Métro:* Concorde)

CARTIER

Cartier has new headquarters and a shop that sells everything, including the entire Must line. Latest in the Must must-have collection: an organizer-*cum*-diary like a Filofax. Never think of Cartier as a source only for jewels—they sell stationery, scarves, leathergoods, dishes, pens, lighters and even the straps for your tank watch. There are small Cartier shops dotted elsewhere around town, like at the Place Vendôme and on the faubourg.

CARTIER
    49 Rue François-1ᵉʳ, 8ᵉ (*Métro:* Franklin D. Roosevelt)

JEAN-CHARLES DE CASTELBAJAC

Castelbajac may be too wild and too expensive for you to make the special trip to this shop slightly off the beaten path, but then, if you even know who he is, you must like this man—so step this way. His creative mind continues to produce original works of art for you to wear when you want the world to notice you. Not for the shy or the short.

JEAN-CHARLES DE CASTELBAJAC

Place du Marché Saint-Honoré, 1er (Métro: Tuileries)

CÉLINE

An old French name that was actually born right after World War II, Céline makes clothes and leathergoods in the manner of Hermès. New ownership has brought new direction to the house, as well as a new shop—with more branch stores anticipated in the world's best shopping cities. (There are already eighty-three stores around the world.) There is a horsey motif, similar to Hermès; scarves, bags and ready-to-wear are the specialty. Prices are less than Hermès, but not by much.

CÉLINE

38 Avenue Montaigne, 8e (Métro: Franklin D. Roosevelt or Alma Marceau)

24 Rue Francois Premier, 8e (Métro: Franklin D. Roosevelt)

26 Rue Cambon, 1er (Métro: Tuileries)

58 Rue de Rennes, 6e (Métro: Saint-Germain-des-Prés)

CHANEL

There's not much to say about Chanel that you don't already know, haven't read or haven't seen on the Broadway stage. Now that Karl Lagerfeld is designing the line, it's even more fun than it was before. The Rue Cambon shop is the couture house and main shop. It's conveniently right behind the Ritz Hotel on a very inconspicuous part of the Rue Cambon. Two small boutiques are open across town but are good to remember if Rue Cambon is mobbed with tourists, as it often is.

There aren't a lot of bargains here, even on sale. A lot of the accessories are put away in black cases, so you have to ask to be shown the earrings and chains, which is no fun and puts a lot of pressure on you. I happen to buy my Chanel at the duty free store at JFK; it's cheaper than in Paris and while you don't get a high fashion selection, you can get simple goldtone earrings—which are always sold out in Paris.

If you're game, try a *used* Chanel suit. A classic is a classic is a classic, no? Check with RÉCIPROQUE or DIDIER LUDOT. Used suits are not cheap, since this is not a new trick. You'll pay $500–$1000 for a good suit. Usually the blouse is sold with the suit at Ludot; at Chanel the blouse is another purchase. Expect to pay $3,000 or more for a new suit at Chanel.

If by any chance you expect to find *faux* Chanel in flea markets, you can forget it right now. France is very strict about copyright laws; Chanel is even stricter. You want a pair of imitation earrings for $20? Go to Manhattan.

CHANEL

31 Rue Cambon 1er (*Métro*: Tuileries), 42 Avenue Montaigne, 8e (*Métro*: Franklin D. Roosevelt or Alma Marceau)

DIDIER LUDOT

24 Galerie Montpensier, Jardin du Palais-Royal, 1er (*Métro*: Palais-Royal)

CHARVET

Although Charvet sells both men's and women's clothing, this is known as one of the grandest resources for men in Continental Europe. Elegant men have been having shirts tailored here for centuries. You may buy off-the-rack, or bespoke. Off-the-rack comes only with one sleeve length, so big American men may need bespoke. The look is Brooks Brothers meets the Continent; traditional yet sophisticated. American men like to come here for status appeal. The mini department store of the shop is filled with *boiserie* and the look of old money. A man's shirt, like all quality men's shirts these days, costs over $100.

CHARVET
      8 Place Vendôme, 1er (Métro: Opéra)

ANDRÉ COURRÈGES

Courrèges has a very traditional basic line, some dynamite skiwear, and very little that is weird or wacky. You still can find some stuff that is so reminiscent of the 1970s that you don't know if it's new or old merchandise, but there are no little white vinyl boots around. Don't laugh because this guy is still strongly in the design business.

ANDRÉ COURRÈGES
      46 Rue du faubourg-Saint-Honoré, 8e (Métro: Concorde)
      40 Rue François-1er, 8e (Métro: Franklin D. Roosevelt)
      49 Rue de Rennes, 6e (Métro: Saint-Germain-des-Prés)
      50 Avenue Victor Hugo, 16e (Métro: Victor Hugo)

CHLOÉ

Years ago Karl Lagerfeld made his fame as the designer for Chloé. He went on to bigger, better and more but has recently returned to his roots when the Dunhill people bought Chloé and wooed back Kaiser Karl. People are talking.

CHLOÉ
      60 Rue du faubourg-Saint-Honoré, 8e (Métro: Concorde)

CHRISTIAN DIOR

Although the real Christian Dior is dead, the line carries on his fashionable tradition. This large house has many floors for shopping—you can get ready-to-wear, costume jewelry, cosmetics, scarves, menswear, baby items and wedding gifts as well as the couture. In fact, several little shops are clustered around the main "house."

One of the best things about the House of Dior is that they seem quite aware that you want to buy from them and have gone out of their way to have items priced for tourists with taste. The gift department is exhaustive—local brides often register here. There are numerous $25–$50 items that will be gift-wrapped for you in the distinctive wrappings that will make your gift list wilt with delight. I give Dior high marks for merchandising their famous name to make everyone happy; I give their salespeople high marks for carrying out the stereotypical haughty behavior that offends many.

CHRISTIAN DIOR

30 Avenue Montaigne, 8ᵉ (*Métro*: Alma Marceau)

DOROTHÉE BIS

The woman responsible for getting this business off the ground was none other than the Duchess of Windsor. Sweaters and knits always have been the house specialty, and continue as such. Prices are moderate to those of us used to outrageously high designer prices. There are several retail outlets: for men, for women, for sports, for discount.

DOROTHÉE BIS

46 Rue Étienne-Marcel, 2ᵉ (*Métro*: Étienne-Marcel)

33 Rue de Sèvres, 6ᵉ (*Métro*: Sèvres-Babylone)

DOROTHÉE BIS STOCK

76 Rue d'Alésia, 14ᵉ (*Métro*: Alésia)

JEAN-PAUL GAULTIER

Difficult decision—to buy Gaultier in Milan, where the shop is easily accessible, or to go out of the way in Paris (well, not too far out of the way) and get the *détaxe*? The Paris shop is fun and worth seeing: it's the cornerstone of the GALERIE VIVIENNE, which is in desperate need of restoration and TLC. Look past the graffiti to soak up the pleasures of the *galerie* itself while you take in the high tech charm of Gaultier's mix of videotech with fashion and architecture, the better to show off his sometimes shocking designs. The younger line is less expensive and not appropriate for anyone over 40. It is sometimes sold at discount shops on Rue Saint-Placide.

JEAN-PAUL GAULTIER
6 Rue Vivienne, 2e (Métro: Bourse or Palais-Royal)

JUNIOR GAULTIER
7 Rue du Jour, 1er (Métro: Les Halles)

MARITHE ET FRANÇOIS GIRBAUD
Masters of the Unisex look, the Girbauds still are making the only clothes that make sense on either sex with equal style. While they have many lines, and you may never even see everything these designers can do, their main store is a must because of the architecture. Discounted jeans can sometimes be found at LE MOUTON À 5 PATTES. Since their most famous commodity is their jeans, I feel compelled to tell you that I buy mine at Filene's Basement in the U.S. for about $30 a pair—this is half the U.S. regular retail price and lower than any discounted price you will find in Paris. Still, Girbaud has status and you should at least look around to take in the latest looks.

MARITHE ET FRANÇOIS GIRBAUD
38 Rue Étienne-Marcel, 1er (Métro: Étienne-Marcel)

COMMUNIQUÉ
8 Rue Saint-Sulpice, 6e (Métro: Saint-Sulpice)

LE MOUTON À 5 PATTES
6 Rue Saint-Placide, 6e (Métro: Sèvres-Babylone)

SOLDES GIRBAUD
5 Rue Planchat, 20e (Métro: Avron)

GIVENCHY
Hubert de Givenchy is the most elegant, handsome man I've ever met. His clothes seem totally

right for Audrey Hepburn and the ladies who lunch, but are not for me. Shopping his stores is a tad confusing—there seem to be shops all over Avenue George V—but it's simple: The couture house is upstairs at 29–31. The men's store takes up three floors and sells everything. The women's things are housed in two separate shops: accessories and clothes Much recent Givenchy ready-to-wear is derivative of Chanel, as is all French *prêt* these days. *Dommage.*

GIVENCHY

3, 8, 29–31 Avenue George V, 8ᵉ (*Métro:* George V)

66 Avenue Victor Hugo, 16ᵉ (*Métro:* Victor Hugo)

HERMÈS

While we're on the subject of status and power, well, I'm just forced to mention Hermès which is perhaps the single best-known French luxury status symbol. The scarf is universally known and coveted; the handbags often have waiting lists. I've personally gone nuts for the enamel bangle bracelets which are tremendously less expensive in Paris than elsewhere in the world—since they cost about the same amount as a scarf, you may want to re-program your mind for a new collectible. Remember, that in order to get the best price at Hermès, you are going to want to qualify for the *détaxe* so plan to buy at least two of anything. Unless you buy a saddle.

You'll have trouble stopping at two if you talking scarves or bangles: there are thousands and thousands of choices. The men's ties are relatively boring, by the way, and cannot compete with the color and design innovation shown in the scarves.

Needless to say, Hermès sells much more than scarves. The saddle department is upstairs at the faubourg shop; the bath towels and porcelains are to the rear. For the person who has everything, the Hermès apron-and-potholder is $100.

Even if you don't plan to buy anything, please come into this shop and give yourself a ten-minute tour; then spritz yourself with Eau de Hermès (appropriate for men or women) and leave—confident that you have seen one of the best stores in the world. Soak up the architecture, the organization of the salons, the people who are shopping, the quality of the goods and most of all—the quality. There is a $10 souvenir book if you just have to have a little something.

Tip: Don't forget to see if your airline sells Hermès scarves in their on-plane shop; these usually cost slightly less than at Hermès (although the selection is often limited). Flying British Air anywhere? They have the lowest prices on Hermès scarves, although the price is in pounds; if the dollar is at $1.75 (or better) you will clean up.

If you want used Hermès, DIDIER LUDOT is the most famous specialist for used Hermès.

HERMÈS
24 Rue du faubourg-Saint-Honoré, 8e (*Métro:* Concorde)

HERMÈS HILTON HOTEL
18 Avenue de Suffren, 15e (*Métro:* Bir-Hakeim)

FABRICE KAREL
If you were a fan of Sonia Rykiel way back when, you will appreciate the knits of Fabrice Karel, which are very similar to old Sonia clothes and a step more sophisticated than Rodier knits—and great for travel. There are a handful of boutiques around Paris, with a few in other French cities. My prediction: Watch as this rising star continues upward. Prices are in the moderate to expensive range; expect to pay $150 for a good sweater. The stock shop has old and current styles; old sells for very little money (how did I pass up that black knit skirt for $40?) while the new collection is less than retail but not dirt cheap. If you wear a lot of navy and white, these

knits are classics to collect. I just love this line, can you tell?

FABRICE KAREL

39 Avenue Victor Hugo, 16e (Métro: Victor Hugo)

95 Rue de Seine, 6e (Métro: Saint-Germain-des-Prés)

FABRIC KAREL STOCK

105 Rue d'Alésia, 14e (Métro: Alésia)

CHARLES JOURDAN

Most famous as a shoe source, this famous French firm also sells clothing and accessories for men and women.

CHARLES JOURDAN

5 Boulevard de la Madeleine, 1er (Métro: Concorde)

KENZO

Yes, Kenzo does have a last name; it's Takada. Yes, Kenzo is a Japanese person—but he is a French designer. The clothes are sold in GALERIES LAFAYETTE, as well as all over the world, and are showcased in big high-tech stores designed to knock your socks off. The line isn't inexpensive—even in the moderate groups—but they have great sales. If you're looking to make one moderate designer purchase, you can get a T-shirt for $30 that will make you feel like a million. See color and fabric used in inventive, creative ways and be inspired.

KENZO

3 Place des Victoires, 1er (Métro: Bourse)

Les Trois Quartiers (mall), 23 Boulevard de la Madeleine, 1er (Métro: Concorde)

18 Avenue George V, 8e (Métro: George V)

99 Rue de Passy, 16e (Métro: Muette)

KENZO STUDIO (ESPACE NOUVEL)

60–62 Rue de Rennes, 6e (Métro: Saint-Germain-des-Prés)

BOUTIQUE LACOSTE

Lacoste is one of those tricky status symbols that you assume will be cheaper in France—after all, it is a French brand. Called *le crocodile* in France, that little alligator has created an international empire and a major brouhaha in counterfeit-land. The popular children's clothes were created for the American market and are not made in France. You will not find the colored, striped single knits, the babywear, or much of the fashion line you are used to at home for sale in France; nor will you beat $13.99 as a U.S. on-sale price for a typical Lacoste short-sleeve polo shirt.

If you buy in France, you will pay $20–$40 for a short-sleeve shirt! A bathing suit may be $50! Kids' windbreakers are $75 to $100! Forget it, honey.

BOUTIQUE LACOSTE

372 Rue Saint-Honoré, 8e (Métro: Concorde)

CHRISTIAN LACROIX

You no longer need to be a couture customer to buy a little something from Christian Lacroix. I found a pin for under $100 worth writing home about. Clothes may be dramatic and expensive but the accessories are wearable and affordable. Walk in to examine everything; the Montaigne space is a visual feast. Get a look at the front of the store. For color and sheer delight, this place should be on everyone's must-see list.

CHRISTIAN LACROIX

26 Avenue Montaigne, 8e (Métro: Alma Marceau)

73 Rue de faubourg-Saint-Honoré, 8e (Métro: Concorde)

KARL LAGERFELD

Yep, it's Kaiser Karl (as *Women's Wear Daily* has dubbed him) and this time he's not into Mademoiselle Chanel's head, nor is he drawing on his sense of who the Chloé customer is—he's just doing his own thing.

KARL LAGERFELD
   19 Rue du faubourg-Saint-Honoré, 8e (*Métro*: Concorde)

LANVIN

The House of Lanvin is one of the oldest and best-known of French couturiers, due mostly to the successful American advertising campaign for their fragrances My Sin and Arpège (Promise her anything...). In recent years, the line has been in transition as the house tries to find its place in the modern world.

LANVIN
   2 Rue du faubourg-Saint-Honoré, 8e (*Métro*: Concorde)

LÉONARD

Léonard is a design house that makes clothes but is perhaps more famous for the prints the clothes are made of. Many pieces are made from a knitted silk; the prints are sophisticated, often floral, and incorporated in ties and dresses. A men's tie will cost about $100, but it makes a subtle statement to those who recognize the print. If you like the fabrics but can't splurge for the couture prices, sometimes you can find yardgoods at the discounter BETTY (see page 105).

LÉONARD
   48 Rue du faubourg-Saint-Honoré, 8e (*Métro*: Concorde)

LOLITA LEMPICKA

Although she sounds like a Polish union leader straight from the docks, she is the darling of the hot set in Paris—and has been for several years. The Lolita Bis line is sold in this store; it's a less expensive (and less wacky) line than her signature collection, and you can buy a jacket in the $350 range. Accessories are extremely affordable and may even come in around $25. Anything from this designer has to be considered collectible by fashion mavens.

Lolita Lempicka

2 bis Rue des Rosiers, 4ᵉ (Métro: Saint Paul)

Lolita Bis

3 bis Rue des Rosiers, 4ᵉ (Métro: Saint Paul)

PHILLIPE MODEL

Have you ever looked at those pictures of the fashion showings (couture and *prêt*) in your WWD or W and fallen in love with the hats that have been teamed with the clothes? If so, you'll be pleased to find Model, who makes many of the hats and who is famous for his inventive, slightly crazy and very stylish *chapeaux*. There are also shoes. This shop happens to be catty-corner to CASTELBAJAC, behind the Hôtel Meurice; there is a more accessible shop in Little Dragons on the Left Bank. Prices on sale are over $100 for a simple hat, but these are the things whimsy is made of. Pascale's mom saw a bunch of out-of-season hats at MI-PRIX, the discounter, for reasonable prices. You just never know.

Philippe Model

33 Place du Marché Saint-Honoré, 1ᵉʳ (Métro: Tuileries)

79 Rue des Saints-Pères, 6ᵉ (Métro: Sèvres-Babylone)

CLAUDE MONTANA

Montana may sound American to us, but these inventive stores and inventive clothes are utterly French.

Claude Montana

31 Rue de Grenelle, 7ᵉ (Métro: Sèvres-Babylone)

3 Rue des Petits-Champs, 1ᵉʳ (Métro: Palais-Royal)

56 Avenue Marceau, 8ᵉ (Métro: Victor Hugo)

THIERRY MUGLER

Count on Mugler for a certain look—both pure and outrageous. The shops offer selling space that could put a museum to shame—walk down a longish entry after you are inside, and into a salon of selling space. Along the way you'll pass blue lights and modern art and a few spare articles of clothing.

THIERRY MUGLER

49 Avenue Montaigne, 8ᵉ (*Métro*: Alma Marceau)

10 Place des Victoires, 2ᵉ (*Métro*: Bourse)

NAFNAF

This is an inexpensive ready-to-wear line. It's young, kicky, very French and works well in suburban America. It's even somewhat affordable. Besides, you may hit a sale or a discount resource as Paris is crawling with this stuff. Note that in British English "naf" means not nice. In French it means hot stuff.

NAFNAF

10, Rue du Jour, 1ᵉʳ (*Métro*: Les Halles)

NEW MAN

New Man jeans have been a unisex standard for over 25 years; the store continues to have the latest fashion trends in jeans for every member of the family. In my opinion, this counts as the French version of The Gap. Prices are *cher*: expect to pay close to $100 for *le denier cri*. As a status item, these can't be beat.

NEW MAN

25–27 Boulevard des Capucines, 1ᵉʳ (*Métro*: Opéra)

BERNARD PERRIS

The clothes are architectural and expensive, but of good quality and high style. Don't be shy— go look at everything. Even if you don't buy, prowl around and soak up the glamour. Dresses begin around $750.

BERNARD PERRIS

48 Rue François-1ᵉʳ, 8ᵉ (*Métro*: Franklin D. Roosevelt)

PALOMA PICASSO

It's possible that Paloma is American, so *excusez moi* if I've messed up, but when your last name is Picasso and your mother is the famous artist François Gilot, it's French enough for me. Paloma's store in Paris is designed by Jacques Grange and showcases all her designs: china, scarves, handbags, cosmetics, gloves—the works. It's a wonderful, chic space that feels almost like a museum; it's perfect for creative people who just want to absorb the wonder's of Paloma's palette.

Note: I bought a Picasso handbag on sale at Bergdorf's for less than in Paris. Those goods that are made in America will be cheaper at home.

PALOMA PICASSO
5 Rue de la Paix, 1er (*Métro*: Tuileries)

NINA RICCI

I think we can cut to the chase here. I mean, we all know Nina Ricci is a couture house. Let's go straight to the good stuff.

Downstairs is where the samples are sold. There is a large and incredible selection of evening gowns, and a few day dresses and suits. If you don't need a ball gown but are looking for a gift to give someone you want to impress, consider the Ricci gift department, which is small enough to consider with one big glance. There are $25 gift items here that will be wrapped in Ricci wrap to ensure that they look like a million. Sale gift items will not be wrapped, by the way. The men's store is next door on the Rue François-1er. This store is closed all day Saturday and from 1 to 2 P.M. every day for lunch.

NINA RICCI
39 Avenue Montaigne, 8e (*Métro*: Alma Marceau)

RODIER

Rodier makes knits that are ideal for travel and I wear a lot of their clothes on the road. Prices in

Paris are no bargain on regular retail but can be good during sales. However, prices at French sales may not be as good as U.S. sale prices! Know your stuff before you pounce. I adore this line; I buy from them annually. Some trips to Paris I score, others are a bust. If you are serious, pay attention to American prices (take notes) before you head to Paris so you can compare. There is some crossover of merchandise from France to the U.S., although you will find different parts of the line in different parts of the world. With batch dying you can extend your wardrobe by adding French pieces, if you find a coordinate you haven't seen in the U.S.

There are sixteen boutiques in Paris, but there's a factory outlet in Woodbury Commons, NY, an outlet mall one hour from Manhattan. Prices in the U.S. are often competitive.

RODIER ÉTOILE
15 Avenue Victor Hugo, 16e (*Métro*: Victor Hugo)

RODIER RIVE-GAUCHE
35 Rue de Sèvres, 6e (*Métro*: Sèvres-Babylone)

RODIER FORUM DES HALLES
1er (*Métro*: Châtelet)

SONIA RYKIEL
Sonia Rykiel began rewriting fashion history when she was pregnant and couldn't find a thing to wear; her children's line was born when she became a grandmother. Now her daughter Nathalie is also designing, so there've been big changes in the family real estate, with Sonia moving into a gorgeous, new store and Nathalie taking over the older space.

It's Nathalie who is responsible for the new line called INSCRIPTION RYKIEL, which is being sold in the former Sonia shop, now that Mom has moved into her new shop right on the Boulevard Saint-Germain.

Inscription Rykiel is a younger, more casual, less expensive line than what Sonia does, and is priced more moderately—though not moderately enough for my taste! Right next door is SONIA RYKIEL ENFANT. The baby clothes are quite sweet but I just couldn't go $50 for a little velour pull on.

Sonia clothes pop up in neat array at RÉCIPROQUE—but because a Sonia design can be worn for only so many years, the items there are often well out of style. Rykiel herself encourages hoarding of her clothes and lots of mixing and matching.

SONIA RYKIEL

70 Rue du faubourg-Saint-Honoré, 8e (Métro: Concorde)

175 Boulevard Saint-Germain, 6e (Métro: Saint-Germain-des-Prés)

INSCRIPTION RYKIEL

6 Rue de Grenelle, 6e (Métro: Sèvres-Babylone)

SONIA RYKIEL ENFANT

4 Rue de Grenelle, 6e (Métro: Sèvres-Babylone)

SR STOCK

64 Rue d'Alésia, 14e (Métro: Alésia)

YVES SAINT-LAURENT

Rive Gauche shops continue to please, and Yves seekers find his new store for couture accessories (jewels downstairs, shoes upstairs) to be one of the most exciting ventures on the faubourg. But prices? Ooh la la. The Left Bank offers several venues for various YSL products: men's, women's and accessories shops abound.

For ready-to-wear that's less expensive than Rive Gauche, there's the Variations line (although if you are a Rive Gauche fan, you may find Variations is too low-end for you). The full Variations line is difficult to find in the U.S. Check it out when you hit the YSL discount store, MENDÈS.

RIVE GAUCHE

    19–21 Avenue Victor Hugo, 16ᵉ (*Métro*: Victor Hugo)

    38 Rue du faubourg-Saint-Honoré, 8ᵉ (*Métro*: Concorde)

    6 Place Saint-Sulpice, 6ᵉ (*Métro*: Saint-Sulpice)

    12 Rond Point des Champs-Élysées, 8ᵉ (*Métro*: Franklin D. Roosevelt)

YSL COUTURE

    43 Avenue Marceau, 8ᵉ (*Métro*: Alma Marceau)

YSL COUTURE ACCESSORIES

    32 Rue du faubourg-Saint-Honoré, 8ᵉ (*Métro*: Concorde)

JEAN-LOUIS SCHERRER

    Scherrer is classic and elegant. If you love an expensive-looking suit, a fabulous silk two-piece, or the look of an international wheeler and dealer, his clothes are for you. The entire collection, couture and ready-to-wear, is on the Avenue Montaigne; there is an additional boutique on the Rue du faubourg-Saint-Honoré. The elegant stone-fronted Montaigne address is high-tech and elegant all at the same time.

    If you love the look but the prices make you wince, there is a shop that sells whatever hasn't moved from the season before. Called the BOUTIQUE DE SOLDES, this shop is so elegant that they hand out those fancy French engraved calling cards! The Boutique de Soldes is not in an especially elegant neighborhood; they have rarely seen an American tourist and speak only spotty English. *Bonne chance.*

JEAN-LOUIS SCHERRER

    51 Avenue Montaigne, 8ᵉ (*Métro*: Franklin D. Roosevelt)

    31 Rue de Tournon, 6ᵉ (*Métro*: Odéon)

    14 Avenue Victor Hugo, 16ᵉ (*Métro*: Victor Hugo)

BOUTIQUE DE SOLDES

29 Avenue Ledru-Rollin, 12ᵉ; Hours: 10 A.M. to 6 P.M.; closed Saturday and Sunday; closed Wednesday in April and August (*Métro*: Ledru-Rollin)

EMANUEL UNGARO

Translate the color of the rainbow through the eyes of a resident of Provence and you get the palette Ungaro is famous for. When the clothes hang in the faubourg-Saint-Honoré shop, you can look in the window and see the colors shimmering in the light. The couture house is a series of three chambers that connect on the Rue Montaigne, so you can see many aspects of the line in one larger space. Don't be afraid to walk in, shoulders back, head held high: take a look.

EMANUEL UNGARO

2 Avenue Montaigne, 8ᵉ (*Métro*: Alma Marceau)

VALENTINO

Valentino shows in Paris and takes his fashion very seriously here. He renovated the shop rather recently in order to hold his place of esteem among his couture neighbors. The Oliver line is also sold here but you will not find any of the Valentino cheapie lines (like V or Night) in this beige marble and glass palace—this is hoity-toity only.

VALENTINO

17–19 Avenue Montaigne, 8ᵉ (*Métro*: Alma Marceau)

LOUIS VUITTON

Louis Vuitton himself opened his first shop in 1854 and didn't become famous for his initials until 1896, when his son came out with a new line of trunks. Things haven't been the same since. The Louis Vuitton shop near the Étoile is nestled off the Arc de Triomphe (around the corner from LE DRUGSTORE PUBLIS) and is a bit hard to find unless you have the street address in your hand;

not to worry, you'll see more than enough when you breeze into the Montaigne flagship.

The Montaigne shop is new, brash, cold and unfriendly. Vuitton staff is there to take you by the hand and guide you to a purchase or two or three. There are set limits on how much you may buy.

Louis Vuitton

57 Avenue Montaigne, 8ᵉ (*Métro*: Alma Marceau or Franklin D. Roosevelt)

Continental Big Names

Despite the fact that the French think French fashion is the best in the world (many other people happen to agree), they have graciously allowed other designers and resources to open up shop in Paris. Of course, the Italians have a good number of shops, representing some of the most famous names in fashion. And many of the world's big fashion names come from other countries, yet show their lines in Paris (VALENTINO, HANAE MORI), and so have come to be considered as French designers.

Paris, like most of continental Europe, has gone crazy for the American look (see page 155). Many U.S. firms have chosen to open branch (and *branche*) shops; many local stores have put their reputation on the line in order to bring American styles to the French public—the entire Chevignon line which includes clothing for both sexes as well as gifts and home styles has gone wild west, Santa Fe and down-home country in their presentations.

GIORGIO ARMANI

Even if you can't afford to buy Armani, you can afford to walk over to the Place Vendôme and stalk through this store. It is one of the most magnificent pieces of architecture you'll see on the retail scene anywhere in the world. The sleek, tailored clothes, for both men and women, are displayed as if in a temple. The Place Vendôme has heretofore been home mostly to the biggest names in jewelry, but Armani, as always, has started a trend.

The EMPORIO shop is a newer wonder for those who feel more casual about prices and life style; there's still nothing very affordable here, but you can still enjoy the high-tech air of chi-chi that you expect to find when you shop with the Armani people.

Note: The Armani shop itself is in the circle part of the sidewalk where the buildings go round; Emporio is on the straightaway as you head toward Opéra. A/X—Armani's answer to The Gap—is so far just an American phenomenon; chances are that Paris will get one in the near future.

GIORGIO ARMANI

6 Place Vendôme, 1er (*Métro*: Tuileries)

ARMANI EMPORIO

25 Place Vendôme, 1er (*Métro*: Tuileries)

LAURA ASHLEY

The French think that the English schoolgirl is acceptably BCBG, so there are eight Ashley shops (if you count the designer showrooms). The most accessible one is on Rue du faubourg-Saint-Honoré; it sells clothing as well as some home furnishing and design elements. Prices are the same as in the U.S. or higher. There are also boutiques in GALERIES LAFAYETTE and AU PRINTEMPS.

LAURA ASHLEY

94 Rue de Rennes, 6e (*Métro*: Rennes)
261 Rue Saint-Honoré, 1er (*Métro*: Concorde)
95 Avenue Raymond Poincaré, 16e (*Métro*: Victor Hugo)

LAURA ASHLEY SHOWROOM

34 Rue de Grenelle, 6e (*Métro*: Rue du Bac)

BOTTEGA VENETA

Bottega in Paris is cheaper than in the United States, but may not be the bargain you were hoping for. They do have huge sales in January and in July, and then you can really clean up. *Détaxe* will make your bargain that much more appealing. This is a new shop located in the heart of the chic shoe and leathergoods shops.

BOTTEGA VENETA
6 Rue du Cherche Midi, 6ᵉ (*Métro:* Sèvres Babylone)

CERRUTI 1881

Nino Cerruti is the Italian designer of this line, which has become a European staple for well-dressed men who fancy the lean, narrow look and elegant color choices. Not for big American bodies or small-town tastes, but otherwise one of the most dashing lines in the world.

CERRUTI 1881
15 Place de la Madeleine, 8ᵉ (*Métro:* Madeleine)

ESCADA

This German line offers expensive sportswear to the French, who adore the look of elegant separates that have a sporty tone with a dressy appeal. You can look casually rich when done up in Escada, but never BCBG. Note that Escada chose to put its lower-priced line Laurel in a shop on the Rue Saint-Honoré, but the Escada store is on the Avenue Montaigne.

ESCADA
418 Rue Saint-Honoré, 8ᵉ (*Métro:* Concorde)
51 Avenue Montaigne, 8ᵉ (*Métro:* Franklin D. Roosevelt)

ESCADA CHEZ MARIE MARTINE
8 Rue de Sèvres, 6ᵉ (*Métro:* Sèvres-Babylone)

LAUREL
402 Rue Saint-Honoré, 8ᵉ (*Métro:* Tuileries)

52 Rue Bonaparte, 6ᵉ (*Métro*: Saint-Germain-des-Prés)

FERRAGAMO

This Italian shoe firm has just recently moved to Paris with a diminutive store in the Little Dragons part of the Left Bank where there happen to be scads of other designer shoe shops. Remember that if you buy two pairs, you'll get the *détaxe*, and the price could be right.

FERRAGAMO

68–70 Rue Saints-Pères, 6ᵉ (*Métro*: Sèvres-Babylone)

GIANFRANCO FERRE

If you don't buy Dior designed by Ferre, you might want to latch on to the master's Italian line, which is what brought him to Paris in the first place. A rather new shop meant to capture the ladies who rarely step out of the 16ᵉ.

GIANFRANCO FERRE

38 Avenue George V, 8ᵉ (*Métro*: George V)

ROMEO GIGLI

Italy's master of cut, romance, whimsy and workable avant-garde clothing has a shop that looks like the chicest airplane hangar in town. Clean white floors, kilim carpets, rafters galore and clothes that float. A must-see; if you taxi directly here you will be in the right part of the Marais for exploring all the best shops and won't have to deal with finding your way from the *métro*.

ROMEO GIGLI

46 Rue de Sévigné, 4ᵉ (*Métro*: Saint Paul)

GUCCI

Gucci has put new effort into getting away from its old image and is promoting itself as a high-fashion resource with top-of-the-line luxury products in top of the line luxury colors. That pink handbag! Be still my heart! Their designs are made in many different countries through various arms of the company, so much of what you see in Europe is not available in the U.S. There are actually two branches of Gucci in a stretch of a few blocks, none offers bargains—the further you get from the faubourg the less you get in terms of atmosphere or crowds. With the *détaxe*, you will save slightly over American prices.

GUCCI

27 Rue du faubourg-Saint-Honoré, 8e (*Métro*: Concorde)

50 Rue Saint-Honoré, 1er (*Métro*: Tuilieries)

JAEGER PF FRANCE

Jaeger is so unmistakably English that it makes me laugh to think of buying it in Paris— but the large, easy-to-shop store is right on the Rue du faubourg-Saint-Honoré, and does a huge business because the conservative tailored clothes appeal to the BCBG set. Designed and furnished exactly like most of the American stores, the Paris Jaeger has prices higher than in London and the U.S., and has the exact same clothes as in the United States for the same time period.

JAEGER PF FRANCE

5 Rue du faubourg-Saint-Honoré, 8e (*Métro*: Concorde)

JOSEPH

Joseph is a British retail genius with a number of stores and design concerns in London; he has one shop on Madison Avenue in Manhattan and several in Paris. The best known Paris shop is on Étienne-Marcel in a string of designer shops with high-tech knock-'em-dead architecture. Prices are higher than in London and range from $100–$300 on an average. The clothes are comfortable, wearable and yet inventive.

JOSEPH

44 Rue Étienne-Marcel, 2e (*Métro*: Étienne-Marcel)

KRIZIA

Italian best-dressed genius Mariuccia Mandelli has brought Krizia to Paris in a large shop that lets the world know she's a contender for your hard-earned savings. The Poi line is a little less expensive than the regular couture line. Prices here are very high, but the look lets the world know that the wearer is exciting, original and ahead of the times.

KRIZIA

27 Rue du faubourg-Saint-Honoré, 1er (*Métro*: Concorde)

LOEWE

Now that the Spanish leather kings at Loewe are owned by a French company (Louis Vuitton Moöt Hennessy), they have moved to Paris and gone for the big impression. Hence this drop-dead chic shop right on the fanciest street in town. The style is Neo-Deco, with granite floors and curving wood walls. Prices for the clothing and leathergoods are about the same as in New York, but with the *détaxe* you may come out ahead.

LOEWE

57 Avenue Montaigne, 8e (*Métro*: Franklin D. Roosevelt or Alma Marceau)

MAX MARA

This Italian master of elegant sportswear that can be affordable but always looks expensive is a welcome addition in Paris—so is the opportunity to get the VAT refund you'll never qualify for in Italy.

MAX MARA

265 Rue Saint-Honoré, 1er (*Métro*: Concorde or Tuileries)

100 Avenue Paul-Doumer, 16e (*Métro*: Muette)

37, Rue du Four, 6e (*Métro*: Saint-Germain-des-Prés)

MCM

This is a German line of leathergoods with little imprints on each piece. They bear a strong resemblance to the LV imprinted line.

MCM
243 Rue Saint-Honoré, 1er (*Métro*: Concorde)

MISSONI

Very modern and fun, the Missoni shop in Paris offers higher prices than Italy but balances them out with a chance at *détaxe*. They have two excellent sales, in July and January—so you may want to wait for them. Even with the benefit of a strong dollar, lower European prices and going without lunch for six months, Missoni still is expensive. Look at T & J VESTOR for Missoni bed linens.

MISSONI
43 Rue du Bac, 7e (*Métro*: Rue du Bac)

T.J. VESTOR
40 Rue Bonaparte, 6e (*Métro*: Saint-Germain-des-Prés)

MOSCHINO

Franco Moschino made his rep as the bad boy of fashion with his humorous salutes to Chanel and other icons. Business has been so good that he's begun to open his own stores, not only in his native Italy but in big-time shopping cities. While his accessories are still carried in specialty and department stores, this is a chance to get the whole statement and to really appreciate just how sharp this guy is. Much is affordable; dresses begin at $150 and top off around $400.

MOSCHINO
68 Rue Bonaparte, 6e (*Métro*: Saint-Germain-des-Prés)

SYBILLA

Sybilla began her design career in France, then left the atelier of Saint-Laurent to return to

Spain (she's part American, part Spanish) and set up shop. Her clothes are famous for their cut and drape. This shop is in an old factory and sells items for the home and bath as well as clothing designs. Between Palais-Royal and Victoires.

SYBILLA
62 Rue Jean-Jacques-Rousseau, 1er (Métro: Louvre)

TRUSSARDI
Prices are only slightly higher than in Italy, and are really quite reasonable for this kind of status canvas and leather accessories; the clothes are very expensive. The store is small but has several salons to wander through.

TRUSSSARDI
21 Rue du faubourg-Saint-Honoré, 8e (Métro: Concorde)

GIANNI VERSACE
Just when the rats began to flee the sinking faubourg, visionary Gianni Versace marched in, took over a prime piece of real estate and turned it into yet another showpiece of architecture and clothing. Every major store this man opens (he has some smaller shops in Paris that aren't as special as this flagship store) is of museum quality. You need to browse just to see what talent can do: the clothes become accessories to the architecture and interior design. Knockoff clothes are a-dime-a-dozen all over the world, but what no one can copy the magic of a space like this.

GIANNI VERSACE
62 Rue du faubourg-Saint-Honoré, 8e (Métro: Concorde)

BOUTIQUE HOMME
67 Rue des Saint-Pères, 6e (Métro: Sèvres-Babylone)

BOUTIQUE FEMME
   64 Rue des Saint-Pères, 6e (Métro: Sèvres-Babylone)

ERMENEGILDO ZEGNA

If you want to spend a lot of money and take
on the suave, sophisticated look of a modern
Count of Monte Cristo, do not miss Zegna, known
for a century in Europe as the maker of the
world's finest wools. The Zegna family runs the
Italian mills that always have provided the best
designers with their wool. A wool jacket or tailored suit from Zegna tells the world you have
arrived (and by Concorde: the plane, not the
métro). Buying in Paris makes sense because of
détaxe.

ERMENEGILDO ZEGNA
   10 Rue de la Paix, 1er (Métro: Opéra)

Oriental Big Names

COMME DES GARÇONS

This Euro-Japanese look is far more Japanese
(as is its designer) and artistic than French and
wearable, but designers and buyers like to look at
the line for its avant-garde notions. Distressed
fashion is only the latest version. Who knows
what's next. Expensive but exciting.

COMME DES GARÇONS
   42 Rue Étienne-Marcel, 2e (Métro: Étienne-Marcel)

HIROKO KOSHINO

The store—and the clothes—are very Japanese, but are so chic that they seem very French.
Hiroko is one of the three Koshino sisters; the
other sisters' clothes are sold at ALMA, not far
away on the Rue du faubourg-Saint-Honoré. The
clean lines of the store and the fastidious elegance of the clothes make this just the kind of

place you want to stare at, whether you can wear (or afford) these clothes or not. Many of the knits are very Western and will fit into your wardrobe. Great sales.

HIROKO KOSHINO

43 Rue du faubourg-Saint-Honoré, 8e (*Métro*: Concorde)

ISSEY MIYAKE

Stark and simple, almost like an art gallery for clothes, this shop in the Marais contains the latest looks from Japan's master, as well as pieces from the Permanent Collection, which are made in limited editions and never go on sale. The regular lines are still sold in shops on the Left Bank.

ISSEY MIYAKE

3 Place des Vosges, 4e (*Métro*: Saint Paul)

17 Boulevard Raspail, 6e (*Métro*: Saint-Germain-des-Prés)

ISSEY MIYAKE HOMME

33 Boulevard Raspail, 6e (*Métro*: Saint-Germain-des-Prés)

MATSUDA

Matsuda clothes are known for their inventiveness; they often influence street fashion as they are adapted and recreated by the students in Paris who can't afford this line.

MATSUDA

26 Boulevard Raspail, 7e (*Métro*: Rue du Bac)

YOHJI YAMAMOTO

Clothes for men and women in the well-cut, but baggy format of comfort and high style.

YOHJI YAMAMOTO

25 Rue du Louvre, 1er (*Métro*: Palais-Royal)

69 Rue des Saints-Pères, 7e (*Métro*: Sèvres-Babylone or Saint-Germain-des-Prés)

JUNKO SHIMADA

Another hotshot Euro-Japanese couture look that is loose and comfortable, but more dressed-up than weird or wild. Simple chic I think they call it.

JUNKO SHIMADA

54 Rue Étienne-Marcel, 2e (*Métro*: Étienne-Marcel)

American Big Names

The second American liberation of Paris began quietly enough when Ralph Lauren opened a shop right at Place de la Madeleine. Now American designers are hustling to open doors to sell the American look. You can see this merchandise at home, and pay less for it; nevertheless, here's a brief blow-by-blow of the Americans in Paris:

ESPRIT

Esprit has tackled several big European cities with a bang—the stores are always masterpieces of design that draw in the crowds, who then can't seem to get enough of the well-priced American clothes. The clothes cost less in the U.S., but then these stores are for Europeans who don't know that—or can't get to the U.S. And then, the clothes that are made in Europe are unique, so there are some winners worth your time. Men's, women's and children's things are for sale, as well as plenty of accessories. This huge store is very avant-garde and exciting to shop.

ESPRIT

9 Place des Victoires, 2e (*Métro*: Bourse)

JOAN & DAVID

Straight from your favorite Ann Taylor store, Joan and David the shoe people have become Joan and David the clothes people. They took over the Rayne shoe store right smack in the middle of Paris' prime shopping area; so they really want you to know that the Americans have landed. Prices are substantially higher than in the U.S.

JOAN & DAVID
   6 Rue du faubourg-Saint-Honoré, 8ᵉ (*Métro:* Concorde)

RALPH LAUREN/POLO

It's all here, just like on Madison Avenue in Manhattan: the fancy woodwork, the gorgeous antiques, the overripe roses in the Chinese porcelain bowl. Men's clothing is downstairs, women's and children's is upstairs. Americans need visit only if they want a laugh—the prices here are so expensive that it makes regular Ralph at retail look like a bargain.

RALPH LAUREN/POLO
   2 Place de la Madeleine, 8ᵉ (*Métro:* Madeleine)

JOSIE NATORI

The queen of American underwear is actually Filipino, but she makes the most luxurious looks in lingerie and has developed enough of an international following to take on the French, who certainly appreciate fine underwear. There is some ready-to-wear as well.

JOSIE NATORI
   7 Place Vendôme, 1ᵉʳ (*Métro:* Tuileries)

CHAPTER SIX

LE SHOPPING

Good Stuff

The essence of French fashion (aside from couture) is simplicity—consider the basic black skirt and white silk blouse—and the way to spruce these basics up has always been through accessories. Hence the importance of the Hermès silk scarf in every French woman's wardrobe. Should you care to go for something more glitzy, these sources offer some of Paris' boldest statements:

BURMA

If the real thing in jewelry and gemstones is beyond you, try Burma! There are a few Burma shops; if you want to have fun while doing this, you stick to the faubourg-Saint-Honoré shop so you can fantasize that you can afford something on this luxury street. Burma knows how to make copies of important jewels.

BURMA

72 Rue du faubourg-Saint-Honoré, 8ᵉ (*Métro*: Concorde or Miromesnil)

KALINGER

While you're roaming the faubourg and looking for drop-dead chic jewelry, make a note to stop in at Kalinger, which is so small you might otherwise miss it. There's more upstairs, so don't worry—tiny space does not mean tiny talent. The flowerpots encrusted with "gems" were the most inventive look I saw in Paris one year. There are also handbags. This is the place for the latest in costume jewelry that's individual, creative, and ahead of its time without being too far-out. The Left Bank shop is bigger, but not as exciting.

KALINGER
60 Rue du faubourg-Saint-Honoré, 8e (*Métro*: Concorde)

KEN LANE
Ken Lane has shops in Paris and London and continues to do well in the *faux* glitz business. His designs are almost obviously imitation and very much the rage right now. Prices are better in the U.S. and you can mail order from the new Fifth Avenue shop in Manhattan. But at least stop and look in the windows. The Saint-Honoré address is the newest shop.

KEN LANE
14 Rue de Castiglione, 1er (*Métro*: Concorde)
249 Rue Saint-Honoré, 1er (*Métro*: Concorde)
50 Rue du Four, 6e (*Métro*: Saint-Germain-des-Prés)

LESAGE
Located in the Schiaparelli space on the Place Vendôme, so it doesn't have a sign you can watch for, Lesage simply says "Lesage" on the windows, with a pink "Schiaparelli" over it. But designer mavens have known for years that Lesage was the house that did all the beading for the couture. This shop, with its "Shocking" interior, where you sit at a little table and trays are brought to you, offers at retail a host of accessories at the highest prices in Paris. Pick from costume jewelery, handbags and even some clothing that is heavily beaded and/or embroidered. The work is sublime, but the price tags are not.

LESAGE
21 Place Vendôme, 1er (*Métro*: Tuileries)

YVES SAINT-LAURENT
Saint-Laurent shows us what he's made of by having the good grace to open a razzle-dazzle shop that allows us to smell the refined air of

couture but still come away with a trophy we can afford—his shop for accessories, which at one time were sold only at The House, has two levels of goodies, many of which are made of crystal and are meant to make your friends very envious that you've been to Paris. Go upstairs for the serious shopping. While the store sells more than jewelry (shoes, sweaters, scarves, ties, etc.), it's the jewelry that gives you an inspiration as to what you should be buying in Paris.

YVES SAINT-LAURENT

32 Rue du faubourg-Saint-Honoré, 8e (*Métro:* Concorde)

SWAROVSKI

This Swiss crystal maker has provided much of the glitter to Lesage over the years, but now has a rather new shop on the Rue Royale where they sell diamond-like jewels made from their top-of-the-line crystals and accessories like handbags with crystal clasps and wine glasses with crystals inserted where the stem meets the bowl. The store—the company's first retail effort on the international scene—is owned by the people who run the CIRO stores (also famous for *faux* baubles).

SWAROVSKI

7 Rue Royale, 8e (*Métro:* Concorde)

Affordable Glitz

ANEMONE, OCTOPUSSY

I have two special resources for costume jewelery and earrings in Paris that are reliable, year after year. Since they are around the corner from each other, they are easy to work. OCTOPUSSY is on the Rue Saint-Honoré, ANEMONE is now on the Rue de Castiglione. It's hard for me to differentiate between the two stores except by their locations, although I think I've been lucky at Octopussy more than at Anemone. They carry a wide range of designer lines as well as many no-name works that are just enough ahead of the times to be worthwhile. Earrings begin around $50 (this is Paris, you know), but may prove to be the best buy of your trip. They will allow you to save up your receipts to qualify for the *détaxe*.

OCTOPUSSY

255 Rue Saint-Honoré, 1er (*Métro*: Tuileries or Concorde)

ANEMONE

7 Rue de Castiglione, 1er (*Métro*: Tuileries or Concorde)

CLEOPATRE

Across from BHV on the side street, not the Rue de Rivoli, this large shop sells obviously fake jewelry and hot fashion looks for few francs. I'm talking teen-time here and really low end, but fun. They have hair ornaments, bracelets, necklaces, pins, and more earrings than you can imagine.

CLEOPATRE

1 Rue du Renard, 4e (*Métro*: Hôtel de Ville)

GAS

Small store with very inventive pieces, often made from odds and ends of memories and souvenirs and beads and doodads all clustered together. More fun than couture in terms of a look; possibly a good investment as a collectible.

GAS

44 Étienne-Marcel, 2e (*Métro*: Étienne-Marcel)

NEREIDES

This is a very south-of-France look, sort of casual and fashiony and resorty with bigger pieces than you might wear to work; various sizes and shapes and a touch of brushed gold and Etruscan influence.

NEREIDES

23 Rue du Four, 6e (*Métro*: Saint-Germain-des-Prés)

Children's Clothes

If you're not the kind of mom—or grandma—who cares to drop a bundle on a single outfit for your little darling, don't forget that the department stores—AU BON MARCHÉ and GALERIES LAFAYETTE are famous for their children's departments. If you like cheap, fun, throwaway things, try PRISUNIC or INNO—each has a toy department and a good selection of inexpensive basics (underwear) and some acceptable ready-to-wear. Not terribly classy, but if you need just a bathing suit or a sweatshirt, why pay more than you have to? If you must have an Yves Saint-Laurent dress for your little princess, buy it at Galeries Lafayette, where you can save the receipt and qualify for *détaxe*.

BONPOINT

For classic styles, you won't find better than Bonpoint and its perfectly crafted outfits. You've never seen anything so superbly made in your life. An adorable romper was $50; a simple smocked dress starts at $100, but prices can go to $300 for the grander stuff. If your child is over five, go upstairs where the fashions for older children are displayed. Parisian women of money and style swear by this resource.

There are several Bonpoint shops all over town, by the way. Some specialize in kids' shoes; one has furniture only. They have some freestanding stores in New York, London, Milan, etc.

If you're impressed with the clothing once you've seen the store but can't hack the prices, perhaps you'd like to try the outlet store where last season's collection (or what's left of it) is sold for a fraction of the uptown price. Here you'll find that $300 little frock for a mere $60! They are closed on Saturday and Sunday. This outlet happens to be convenient to life on the Left Bank, so go for it.

BONPOINT
15 Rue Royale, 8ᵉ (*Métro*: Madeleine)

BONPOINT SOLDES
82 Rue de Grenelle, 7ᵉ (*Métro*: Rue du Bac)

TARTINE ET CHOCOLAT
Maternity dresses and layettes, French style, both classic and *nouveau*. My own fave: the big pink hippo in pink and white stripes sitting in a playpen and begging to be taken home to someone's child. There are Tartine et Chocolat boutiques in the major department stores. Some duty frees (like SILVER MOON) sell the kiddie toiletry line, which makes a nice gift.

TARTINE ET CHOCOLAT
89 Rue du faubourg-Saint-Honoré, 8ᵉ (*Métro*: Concorde)

PETIT FAUNE
Very original baby clothes in the *nouveau* style—some have matching shoes and hats. Everything is very, very small—up to size 2. The clothes are very American, and even the fanciest isn't in the classic style.

PETIT FAUNE
33 Rue Jacob, 6ᵉ (*Métro*: Saint-Germain-des-Prés)

Fabrics, Notions and Crafts

For those who sew, Paris, the home of fancy seams, offers plenty to get creative with. While fabric may not be less expensive than at home, the selection in Paris is so incredible that you are unable to think about price at all. Besides couture fabrics, you'll find the trendy fabrics—imitations of the hottest looks to hit Europe that Americans are still reading about in WWD. When the Gianni Versace-style prints went crazy a while back, I was able to buy a washable polyester with a silky hand to make a skirt—total cost of the project was $25.

No one in the States had anything to compete.

Should you be somewhat interested in fabric, but do not want to spend much time tracking it down, stop by BOUCHARA, which is next door to all the big department stores in the 9e and has both home furnishings fabrics and notions as well as tons of fabric choices, many of them moderately priced.

If you want a taste of the couture, or a silly adventure, you may want to spend a few hours in the Marché Saint-Pierre area (18th *arrondissement*). You can combine this with a little tourist activity by walking up the back side of Montmartre to Sacré-Coeur, visiting the famous church, and then taking the funicular down. When you get out of the tram you will be in a neighborhood that sells fabrics, notions, etc. Couture ends are sold; shopkeepers are friendly. Some working knowledge of French will be helpful. Cash. If you are going straight there, ask the taxi driver to take you to Marché Saint-Pierre, 2 Rue Charles-Nodier, 18e. This will be a pricey taxi ride, by the way—the 18e is pretty far out. You can go on the *métro*, of course. (Métro: Anvers)

For a few other couture fabric resources, try these sources which are justifiably famous for their fabric selections—Chanel, YSL, Dior, the whole shooting match. ARTISANAT is in the Sentier, and also sells wool and yarn goods. SEVILLA is right off Passy and is fabulous, if you hit it. Please remember that couture fabrics are not inexpensive—often they are $50 a yard for a silk that may not even be very wide. Bouchara carries the good stuff but is more famous for its wide range of copycat fabrics at good prices.

ARTISANAT TEXTILE, 21 Rue des Jeúneurs, 2e (Métro:'Sentier)

LA SOIE DE PARIS, 14 Rue d'Uzès, 2e (Métro: Rue Montmartre)

SEVILLA, 38 Rue de l'Annonciation, 16e (Métro: Muette)

LE STAND DES TISSUS, 11 Rue de Stein-
kerque, 18ᵉ (*Métro*: Anvers)

RODIN, 36 Champs-Élysées, 8ᵉ (*Métro*: Franklin
D. Roosevelt)

BOUCHARA, 54 Boulevard Haussmann, 9ᵉ
(*Métro*: Chaussée Antin)

If you're just looking for fabrics and notions,
but do not need top-of-the-line couture materials, these two sources are great fun to
browse:

LA DOUGUERIE

This is not a couture fabric source but a store
for yarn, buttons, ribbons, feathers, crafty bric-a-
brac and stuff, but it is so visual and exciting that
anyone who knits or sews will swoon with delight.
It's on a good street for boutique-hopping and is
right outside the FORUM DES HALLES mall. You
can easily get here as you walk from MENDÈS, the
YSL jobber toward the mall.

Lᴀ Dᴏᴜɢᴜᴇʀɪᴇ
9–11 Rue du Jour, 1ᵉʳ (*Métro*: Les Halles)

LES PASSEMENTERIES DE CLAUDE DECLERCQ

Giving new meaning to the term French dressing, this shop full of trimmings allows you to have
all the finishings for fabrics and upholstery that
make it French—ruffles, *passementerie*, rosettes in
rows, etc. Some old; most new. There is nothing
like this at your local mall.

Lᴇs Pᴀssᴇᴍᴇɴᴛᴇʀɪᴇs ᴅᴇ Cʟᴀᴜᴅᴇ Dᴇᴄʟᴇʀᴄǫ
15 Rue Étienne-Marcel, 1ᵉʳ (*Métro*: Étienne-
Marcel)

Makeup and Perfume Tips

Perfume and makeup are possibly the best
buys in Paris. I'm talking French brands here. This
rule is not set in stone (see page 8). Yet you can
score such gigantic savings if you understand the

ins and outs of the system. There will be a quiz next Friday.

- Makeup in France is different from French makeup in the U.S. Makeup (even French brands) sold in the United States is made in the United States according to FDA specifications or shipped to the U.S. in accordance with FDA specifications—therefore contents and colors will vary between home and France. Names of products may be the same or different. Makeup with the same name may not be identical in shade.

- French perfume is also different in France than in the U.S., mainly because it is made with potato alcohol (yes, you can drink it—just like Scarlett O'Hara) while Anglo-Saxon countries use cereal alcohol. Potato alcohol increases the staying power of the fragrance, as well as the actual fragrance—to some small degree. If you've ever shopped for perfume in the Caribbean you know that certain stores make a big brouhaha over the fact that they import directly from France. Now you know why that's important. The French version is considered the best version—the "real" version.

- Many American brands you see in France are made in France (or Europe) for the European market—such as Estée Lauder and Elizabeth Arden. You may save on these items when *détaxe* is credited to your purchase, but generally you do not save on American brands in Europe.

- If you ship your beauty buys, you automatically get a 40% discount; you need not buy 1,200 francs worth of merchandise. But the cost of postage can be high on beauty products that are in heavy jars. This is a fine point over which you may have to have heated discussions with some dutyfree proprietors. It is the law. If you ship one tiny mascara out of France, you can get the 40% discount. You won't save anything, but you can get the discount.

- French perfumes are always introduced in France before they come out internationally. This lead time may be as much as a year ahead. If you want to keep up with the newest fragrances, go to your favorite duty free and ask specifically for the newest. If you are stumped for a gift for the person who has everything, consider one of these new fragrances.

- The amount of the basic discount, not the *détaxe*, varies from one shop to the next, as does the system by which you gain your refund. Ask in several shops and find a program that you feel comfortable with; or simply go for a flat discount and avoid the fuss.

Sitting Pretty

BOURJOIS

Now then, about Bourjois. Many years ago, when I was a snob, I did not dare admit to anyone that I discovered a fabulous cheap makeup at Dames de France in Le Mans. It was only years later, when I worked on the set of the television show *Dallas* and the makeup man told me he used this brand, that I thought I could be onto something. Then—get this—I learned from a big-name designer that Bourjois is made by the same company that makes the Chanel makeup, and is virtually the same thing. (Bourjois actually owns the Chanel line as a subsidiary.)

Bourjois is hard to find in the U.S. since only Galeries Lafayette in New York carries it, but it's not hard to find in Paris if you know where to look. Forget the duty frees; buy Bourjois at any

PRISUNIC, at SEPHORA, at GALERIES LAFAYETTE or any big department store. They even sell it at the duty free at Orly Sud! Prices are the same in all retail outlets; it's two francs less at the duty free.

Now then, what makes the line so special? For starters: many, many, many shades of eyeshadow sold in big containers that can last you forever. Nail polish and lipsticks are also good. Rouge colors are excellent. Mascara is boring but cheap; their liquid makeup may be nice but I use the creamy thick kind (from Chanel) which Bourjois does not make. Many of the shades in the Chanel line and the Bourjois line are exactly the same; I've matched them up myself. They do have different names.

BOURJOIS MAKEUP

in department stores; Prisunic, Inno

ANNICK GOUTAL

Putting Annick Goutal and BOURJOIS together sort of jumps you from the ridiculous to the sublime—as mass-merchandised as SEPHORA is, that's how elite and unique Goutal is. Sold from a tiny shop on the Rue de Castiglione, there are actually a number of outlets for the product in Paris and a growing number around the world. It's sold at Bergdorf's in New York and Harrod's in London. So what's so special? Just step into the Belle Epoque-style salon and sniff the house brands which include perfumes, lotions and house scents. The new men's eau de toilette is a winner. If you are looking for a special gift for someone who understands the meaning of the word sublime, search no further. Look at the firm logo spelled out in a mosaic in the sidewalk in front of the store.

ANNICK GOUTAL

14 Rue de Castiglione, 1er (*Métro*: Tuileries or Concorde)

GUERLAIN

Perhaps the most famous name in fragrance in France, Guerlain has two different types of boutiques in Paris: some sell products only, others have salons on the premises. Some insider's information: Guerlain perfumes are sold only through Guerlain stores, and are not discounted; the brand is rarely found at a duty free. If you see it at a duty free, chances are there is no discount. Also note that only some of the fragrances are sold in the U.S. There is also a complete makeup line. An annual price list for fragrance and all products is printed; pick one up at any boutique so you can compare to your U.S. price list.

GUERLAIN BOUTIQUES

68 Avenue Champs-Élysées, 8e (*Métro*: Franklin D. Roosevelt) Tel.: 47-89-71-00

2 Place Vendôme, 1er (*Métro*: Opéra)

93 Rue de Passy, 16e (*Métro*: Muette)

29 Rue de Sèvres, 6e (*Métro*: Sèvres-Babylone)

35 Rue Tronchet, 8e (*Métro*: Madeleine)

GUERLAIN INSTITUTS DE BEAUTÉ

68 Avenue Champs-Élysées, 8e (*Métro*: Franklin D. Roosevelt)

29 Rue de Sèvres, 6e (*Métro*: Sèvres-Babylone)

PERLIER

This beauty line is made with honey and is widely sold in the U.S. In fact, sometimes I can buy it at discount prices at Marshall's and save on the French price. The nice thing about the line is that they have adorable little yellow shops and small size samples and honey bath balls that are great for gifts. There's all sorts of beauty products, shampoos, bath gels and creams, honey milk body lotion, morning cream, body lotion, day cream...you're getting the idea, I can tell.

PERLIER

8 Rue de Sèvres, 7e (*Métro*: Sèvres-Babylone)

SEPHORA

This is a chain of cosmetics shops that now are all over France. There's one about a block from the discount stores on Rue Alésia, but in the opposite direction (only a block); another is near the big Boulevard Haussmann department stores in the 9e. There's also one in the FORUM DES HALLES which may be reason enough to enter this major mall space. You can also bump into one elsewhere—like the next time you are in Provence or Biarritz.

Sephora is not a discounter and gives only the *détaxe*, not the duty-free price. So you'd have to spend a lot to get a price reduction; certainly this is the store to tempt you to do so. It is always a huge shop, with counter after counter of makeup and a small department of underwear and panty-hose in the far back. All brands are carried here, including BOURJOIS (see page 166), as well as dime-store brands you have never heard of, and big-name lines. There's also a bath section, where you can get some very nice bath gels for $10 a jar (the jar is heavy but makes a splendid gift) and bath crystals. I have to be honest with you: it doesn't make sense for a tourist to shop here, because you will forfeit the 20% duty-free discount, but many, many lines here are not sold in the duty-free stores. Sometimes you just have to throw common sense to the wind. Calling *le mistral*.

SEPHORA

2e (Métro: Châtelet or Les Halles)

50 Rue de Passy, 16e (Métro: Muette)

66 Rue de la Chaussée d'Antin, 9e (Métro: Trinité)

38 Avenue du Général-Leclerc, 14e (Métro: Alésia)

SHU UEMURA

He's one of the most famous makeup artists in the world; his makeup products are sold all over the world and he's a cult hero in his native Japan. Color is the name of the game here. The hues are spectacular. If you consider yourself an aficionado of cosmetics, to be in Paris and not go to Shu Uemura is a sin. Yes, it's even better than Bourjois; more expensive too. A single square of color costs about $16. Splurge. High-tech shop is filled with samples and mirrors and brushes and encourages you to come in and make up your face again and again.

SHU UEMURA

176 Boulevard Saint-Germain, 6e (*Métro*: Saint-Germain-des-Prés)

Makeup Duty Frees

Ever since Catherine, the duty free in the Hôtel Meurice, went out of business, I have struggled to find a substitute. Instead, I've found several different kinds of deals and many options. Not every duty free operates the same way, so you might want to try a few, see what they have and where the vibes feel best. I happen to like small stores, but I also have to go on reputations and whispered facts that come from my duty free friend in the Caribbean, Roger Albert.

Please note: The amount needed to qualify for *détaxe* has gotten quite hefty and could even rise. As it is, there is some variation between shops— so ask first. The average is 2,000 francs but some stores are now pegged at 2,500 FF! You are looking at plunking down $400 in order to save money. So look before you leap.

Announcement: If all the details of the *détaxe*, the discount, the 13-or-is-it-16%, the 20%-or-is-it-the-40%?, make you nuts, throw in the towel and go to a duty free which offers a flat discount to every customer regardless of how much you buy. It's pretty easy to find one that gives a 25% flat discount, especially if you pay cash; I even found one that gives a 30% flat discount and lets you pay with plastic!

BENLUX

Benlux is one of the most famous duty frees, located across the street from both the Louvre and the Hôtel du Louvre. This store has three or four floors of goods including clothes; one floor is strictly for Japanese customers: all the signs are in Japanese, all the sales help is Japanese. Very exclusive. While they have a large selection and a big reputation, I find the store too big and too impersonal. You choose at one counter, pay at another and then return for your items—when the store is crowded this can ruin your nerves.

BENLUX
174 Rue de Rivoli, 1er (*Métro*: Palais-Royal)

CASTY

Casty is my choice for a big haul because they are located across the street from where the Catherine shop was and competition with Catherine forced them into a refund style which is the best in Paris. When you qualify for the *détaxe* at Casty, they will charge you 40% less on your credit card right out. If they do not receive the executed *détaxe* papers, they will charge you the additional fee later on. But you'd be a fool not to process the papers, so you have the benefit of not paying out extra money or waiting for a refund. Very few stores do this.

The shop is medium-sized and quite fancy; it's beneath the Intercontinental Hotel with its front door right near the hotel's main entrance; it's convenient to the whole world of shopping. Aside from all the big brands of perfume and cosmetics, they carry some accessories. They are trying to absorb Catherine's customers, so stay tuned. You must spend 2,000 francs to qualify for *détaxe*; there is a 20–25% flat discount if you do not go the *détaxe* route, depending on the brand (Chanel is a 20% discount).

CASTY

3 Rue de Castiglione, 1er (*Métro*: Concorde or Tuileries)

HELENE DALE

I found this famous duty free because of the swarm of husbands standing out front. Inside the long narrow shop there were tons of products, tons of salesgirls and tons of customers. I considered running out screaming, but they were doing such brisk business that I was fascinated. This is a favorite resource for Japanese tourists; Roger Albert also recommends it. I bumped into the branch across the street from Le Grand Hotel Intercontinental; there is another branch on Saint-Honoré.

HELENE DALE

37 Boulevard des Capucines, 2e (*Métro*: Opéra); 253 Rue Saint-Honoré, 1er (*Métro*: Tuileries or Concorde)

PARFUMERIE CHAMPS-ÉLYSÉES

Do not ask too many questions here, especially the obvious one: like why this store is NOT located on the Champs-Élysées. It doesn't matter. You'll be delighted to find it because it offers everything you want in a duty free: it's small and personal; the sales people are friendly; they give you a generous amount of samples when you buy something; they have everything including Chanel and they take plastic. Now for the good news: this is the store that offers a flat 30% discount to everyone with a foreign passport. This could be my single best tip this trip.

PARFUMERIE CHAMPS-ÉLYSÉES

8 Rue Royale, 8e (*Métro*: Concorde)

RAOUL & CURLY

One of the most famous of the big-name duty-free shops, Raoul & Curly is always jammed. It's also tiny but they have everything, including a gigantic selection of cosmetics. We're talking floor-to-ceiling stock. Downstairs there are some gift items, such as men's shirts and ties and some women's handbags. Frankly, the place leaves me cold; I mention it because they have an excellent reputation and an easy-to-get-to location.

RAOUL & CURLY

47 Avenue de l'Opéra, 2e (*Métro*: Opéra)

SILVER MOON

I can't help but be attracted to Silver Moon even though I'm not sure why. Essentially it's no different from any other place in town—yet the mere fact that it's spacious makes an American feel at home. The location in the mini-mall LES TROIS QUARTIERS gives you a reason to try the mall; their star card program may offer you further discounts. This happens to be a large chain with stores all over town—so you can go from one to the next and use your star card to run up another 5% discount. The basic discount is 20%.

SILVER MOON

Les Trois Quartiers, 23 Boulevard Madeleine, 1er (*Métro*: Madeleine)

MICHEL SWISS

Another of the fabulously famous duty-frees. This one is upstairs in a building whose elevator can take only three adults. In the high season, tourists stand in line in the courtyard just waiting to get into the elevator! The selection is immense; so are the crowds. This is a great resource for the person who may not spend much and wants to get *détaxe* without going to a department store. The discounts and *détaxe* vary from product to product and may confuse you a tad.

MICHEL SWISS

16 Rue de la Paix, 2e (*Métro*: Opéra)

Hairstylists

I've taken to having my hair done when I travel—not only does it save on the stress of packing several hairdryers of different voltages, but it allows me into a new world for a few hours and a chance to see how the other half lives. I come away with a lot more than clean hair.

CARITA

Perhaps the most famous name in beauty in all of Paris, Carita offers an entire townhouse devoted to putting Madame's best foot forward. The entrance is on the faubourg, but off the street; the door is a wall of glass with an electronically controlled wave machine so that the ocean seems to separate you from the world beyond. Indeed, more than an ocean separates some of us from Carita's kind of style.

The great thing about this place, aside from the fact that the reception people speak English, is that it's so organized you can be assured you'll be taken care of. Just walk in to the appointment clerk (around to the left on the street level after you've parted the waves) and make an appointment. Since you probably don't have a regular stylist you take whomever you get; but you're safe here at Carita so it doesn't matter. I have a different stylist each time; some don't speak English. It doesn't matter; sign language will work or someone else at another station will translate.

The stylist are all dressed in white uniforms; the patrons are wearing expensive clothes and carrying the best handbags in Paris. Attached to each handbag is a medallion you are given when you check in; it's your client number which stays with you until you pay the bill.

Note: Patrons do not take off their clothes here; the smock is put on directly over what you are wearing. Check your coat and totebags on the main floor. You will be pampered like a princess.

The cost of the pampering is the going rate for ultra fancy in Paris; you can do better price-wise. But never experience-wise. A shampoo and blowdry, tip is included, costs about $40.

Beauty products and accessories are sold at the back desk on the street floor. Knowing who Carita is and having something the salon in your purse is big status.

There's a men's floor; you can walk in and make an appointment or call or fax ahead. Phone: 42-65-79-00; fax: 47-42-94-98. My last appointment was with Cecile. She didn't speak English, but gave me the coiffure on the cover and a hairstyle that lasted a week.

CARITA

11 Rue du faubourg-Saint-Honoré, 8e (*Métro*: Concorde)

JACQUES DESSANGE

Still famous after all these years, Dessange has a number of shops in Paris and other locations. To get the salon most convenient to you call 46-04-37-27 in Paris, or ask your concierge, who can also book your appointment. Not quite as fancy as Carita, but with a big time reputation nonetheless, Dessange has a younger clientele who might want a more with-it approach than traditionalist CARITA will provide. Hollywood's Jose Eber started here. Sometimes you can run into a promotional package where the shampoo, cut and dry costs 195 francs! They may also give a free makeup consultation. There is a beauty and makeup line; you'll know it by the JD monogram. This line is sold at the salons and at pharmacies.

JACQUES DESSANGE

37 Franklin D. Roosevelt, 8e (*Métro*: Franklin D. Roosevelt)

SALON GREGOR

If you are looking for a little neighborhood place with no fancy reputation, no fancy prices and no extra fuss—just a nice place in an easy-to-get-to location—Gregor could be what you are looking for. This small, but hip, neighborhood salon is open on Monday (not all beauty salons are) as well as Thursday evenings. Prices are half of CARITA's. (Telephone: 47-03-39-59)

SALON GREGOR
342 Rue Saint-Honoré, 1er (*Métro*: Tuileries)

MANIATIS

Still one of the hot shops for models and runway stars, Maniatis has three salons and a beauty school at the FORUM DES HALLES where you can sign up for a free haircut if you're willing to let a student practice on you. To get info on the training session call 47-20-00-05—in these sessions they'll take men, women and teens; Wednesday evenings.

MANIATIS
35 Rue de Sèvres, 6e (*Métro*: Sèvres-Babylone)

Shoes and Leathergoods

Shoe freaks will find the Little Dragons neighborhood of the Left Bank (page 80) a treasure trove of little shoe stores belonging to famous designers and hoping-to-be-famous designers. Weave along these streets and you can't go wrong. CHARLES JOURDAN, perhaps the biggest name in French shoes, has branched into ready-to-wear and is listed with French designers (page 126), as is HERMÈS, VUITTON, etc. I've left out the mainstays here and concentrated on the smaller and lesser known but knockout talents. And then I threw in a few discount sources. Other discount sources (page 104) have shoes and handbags, especially TANGARA.

CHAUSSURES DE LUXE

Just like the name says, they sell deluxe shoes here. But discounted! They are last year's shoes, *mais oui*, but most of them are from Charles Jourdan. The store is tiny, the curved staircase down is even tinier, but there you can find Charles Jourdan silk scarves (the huge shawl size) for about $100, and even deluxe designer underwear. Kids' shoes too. This is only slightly off the beaten track and may be worth a quick hit if you are a shoe freak. They open at 10:30 A.M.

CHAUSSURES DE LUXE

2 Rue de l'Arc de Triomphe, 7e (*Métro*: Étoile; RER: Charles de Gaulle)

DELVAUX

Straight from Belgium and so stunning that you should consider this for your first stop if you are looking for either a handbag or an architect (the store is also gorgeous), this line is deluxe, yet practical, with many bags large enough to fit into an active American life. Prices are in the $200–$400 range, which somehow seems like a bargain for this kind of quality and luxury. A fine status tool for the person who wants something no one else at home can get.

DELVAUX

18 Rue Royale, 8e (*Métro*: Concorde)

STÉPHANE KELIAN

A famous name in shoes with stores all over Paris, and the world, Kelian has been able to successfully combine a hotshot mentality with shoes that work and are comfortable to wear.

STÉPHANE KELIAN

6 Place des Victoires, 2e (*Métro*: Bourse)

MAUD FRIZON

Maud Frizon is made in Italy but designed in France and sold in a handbags-only shop on the Rue de Grenelle on the Left Bank and at a shoe store on the Rue des Saints-Pères.

If you crave "Maudies" but find them out of your budget, try Miss Maud, or go discount (see Mi-Prix, page 109).

MAUD FRIZON

7 Rue de Grenelle, 7e (*Métro*: Sèvres-Babylone)

81–83 Rue des Saints-Pères, 7e (*Métro:* Sèvres-Babylone)

Miss Maud, 21 Rue de Grenelle, 7e (*Métro:* Sèvres-Babylone)

CHRISTIAN LOUBOUTIN

One of the new shoe darlings for those with diamonds on their souls (or soles), Louboutin has made his mark with wacky designs from heels that look like handcarved trees, to shoes that spell fame and fortune. Prices begin at $300; many celebrity clients. Located in one of the best arcades in town.

CHRISTIAN LOUBOUTIN

Vero-Dodat (arcade), 19 Rue Jean-Jacques Rousseau, 1er (*Métro:* Louvre)

DIDIER LAMARTHE

If you are looking for something drop-dead French—elegant and *sportif* and totally different from the other big names sold in duty frees and American department stores—head for this small shop on the faubourg, where luggage, handbags, and small leathergoods (wallets, etc.) are sold at top-of-the-line prices to those who buy only the best.

DIDIER LAMARTHE

219 Rue Saint-Honoré, 1er (*Métro:* Tuileries)

LA MALLE BERNARD

For a different kind of chic altogether, find Le Grand Hotel Intercontinental and look directly across the street from the front door. This store specializes in a casual kind of elegance that is similar to Dooney & Bourke in the U.S., but is much more expensive. There's canvas plus leather, or leather with leather; the weekend bags and totes are the most stunning. Examples of French class.

LA MALLE BERNARD

3 Rue Scribe, 9e (*Métro:* Opéra)

MAXBALLY

I have not listed Bally shoes with the thought that you know enough about Bally shoes to find a shop on your own or walk in when you pass one. But attention trendsetters: Bally has begun a relatively new international chain of shoe stores to sell younger and more high-fashion-oriented shoes to teens and tweens (and me too). Prices are lower; style is almost high-tech on casual items but there is also dress-up; they carry big sizes for women; they have men's shoes too. For $50 I found a fabulous pair of suede shoes.

MAXBALLY

16 Rue de Sevres, 7e (*Métro*: Sèvres-Babylone)

LEO MILLER

If you can't hack the pricetag on an Hermès Kelley bag, but are convinced you must have one anyway, amble on over here—a few short blocks from Hermès—where they have pretty good imitations (alright, awfully good) and pretty fair prices. Lots of colors; other styles too.

LEO MILLER

12 Rue de Castiglione, 1er (*Métro*: Concorde)

RENAUD PELLEGRINO

It was Maggie Sheerin, queen of the handbags, who turned me on to this secret source rumored to make designs for Hermès. In the in-between years, Pellegrino has become a legend in his own time: he's carried in big-time U.S. stores and has moved into spiffy headquarters on my favorite street, while still maintaining his first shop in the Little Dragons area of the Left Bank. His work is characterized by a combination of color and panache. The quality is the same as Hermès, but there's more humor here. Custom work is welcome. Look for special shapes and color combinations and something a little more unusual than a Kelley-style bag—although you can get that as well. Prices begin at $250.

RENAUD PELLEGRINO

348 Rue Saint-Honoré, 1er (Métro: Tuileries); 15 Rue du Cherche-Midi, 6e (Métro: Sèvres-Babylone)

CAMILLE UNGLIK

My notes are very simple. They say: Fab shoes!!! on the back of the card. The store is small; it's in the Little Dragons area. The shoes are inventive and whimsical so that if you only bought one thing in Paris to show off at home, these shoes would be it.

CAMILLE UNGLIK

66 Rue des Saints-Pères, 6e (Métro: Sèvres-Babylone)

Foodstuffs/Picnics

If you are looking for an inexpensive gift to bring home, consider taking home a small but tasty treat or even putting together your own food basket. Foodstuffs are not necessarily easy to pack or lightweight, but they can be rather cheap and look like a lot once you get home and put them in your own basket or wrap in a clever fashion.

My single best gift is a jar of mustard (not just any jar, mind you: Maille's "Provençale"—it's orange). A selection of four mustards (total cost in France, $6) makes a great hostess or housewarming gift.

The easiest place to do foodstuff shopping, and probably the cheapest, is at PRISUNIC or MONOPRIX. There's a Prisunic on the Champs-Élysées, and a Monoprix next door to GALERIES LAFAYETTE, so both are convenient to tourists. FELIX POTIN is a chain of popular grocery stores—some are teeny tiny, others are pretty large. Ask your hotel concierge where the nearest one is upon arrival—this is where you can buy bottled water, Coca-Cola, fruit, etc.

If your palate or your pocketbook are advanced, Paris has no shortage of food palaces like FAUCHON, HEDIARD, etc. As far as I'm concerned the grocery store next to AU BON MARCHÉ (LA GRANDE ÉPICERIE) and the one above Monoprix on Boulevard Haussmann (LAFAYETTE GOURMET) are more reasonably priced than the more famous houses and more fun to shop. Don't forget the entire Rue du Buci with two grocery stores and many small shops.

You cannot bring back any fresh foods; processed hard cheeses are legal, all others are not. Dried items (such as mushrooms) are legal; fresh fruits and veggies are not.

If you plan on buying foodstuffs, save your plastic bags from shopping adventures or bring a boxful of Baggies with you. Wrap each jar or bottle in plastic and tie the top of the bag with a twist-tie before you pack the item. If the cushion provided by your clothes doesn't protect the jar, at least you won't get mustard all over your new suede shoes. Many of the big food stores will ship for you, but beware: Foodstuffs usually are very heavy.

LA BOUTIQUE LAYRAC TRAITEUR

Anything from *boeuf bourguignon* to *pommes de terre au gratin* dished out in a container for your picnic or party. A fancy pigeon dish may be $10 a serving, but the potatoes are only $4. Little is over $15, the prices are quite fair. Who needs Tour d'Argent?

LA BOUTIQUE LAYRAC TRAITEUR
29 Rue de Buci, 6e (*Métro*: Saint-Germain-des-Prés or Mabillon)

FAUCHON

Prices are high here, and many of these items are available elsewhere (have you been to a Prisunic or Inno lately?), but it's a privilege just to stare in the windows. The salespeople also are extraordinarily nice. There are three parts to the store: Fruits and dry goods are in a mini-department store of many floors, prepared foods are next door, and the cafeteria is across the street. You buy a ticket, then get the food.

FAUCHON

26 Place de la Madeleine, 8ᵉ (*Métro*: Madeleine)

FLO PRESTIGE

This is actually a small chain and also a catering service. They can cater for me any day. I buy prepared foods, cakes and even ice cream here. They have their own line of soups and canned goods; you can buy complete meals and enjoy a gourmet dinner for less money than in a restaurant. Their prepared meals will make you wish your hotel supplied your room with a microwave. I use the shop off Rue Saint-Honoré because it's near all three of my usual hotels; I trust all their stores. They also own a group of famous restaurants.

FLO PRESTIGE

42 Place du Marché Saint-Honoré, 1ᵉʳ (*Métro*: Tuileries)

61 Avenue de la Grande Armée, 16ᵉ (*Métro*: Argentine)

102 Avenue du President Kennedy, 16ᵉ (*Métro*: Passy)

FOUQUET

If asked to pick the single best gift item in Paris, I just might say it's the box of ten jars of goodies from Fouquet. Fouquet gift boxes are as heavy as they are famous, but the store will ship for you. There's no problem finding lovely gifts in the $25 to $50 range, but the shipping may double the price. Still, the boxes are so extravagant that it does seem worth it. Jars are filled with chocolates, jams, gingered fruits, nuts and assorted edibles.

FOUQUET
    22 Rue François-1er, 8e (Métro: Franklin D. Roosevelt)

G-20 COMESTIBLES
    More like a fancy supermarket, G-20 is right smack in the middle of the Rue de Buci and the stalls and flowers and fresh produce and French charm of the Left Bank. Stock up from the vendors and the market and have a marvelous picnic. This store is bigger than a 7-11 but not as big as a supermarket. If you don't want to shop at this type of grocery store, or from the vendors of fresh goods, you still are almost next door to LA BOUTIQUE LAYRAC TRAITEUR for prepared foods.

G-20 COMESTIBLES
    Rue de Buci, 6e (Métro: Saint Germain or Mabillon)

GARGANTUA
    Another of my regulars between the Hôtel du Louvre and the Meurice, Gargantua has cooked foods, wines, jars, and cans of fine eats. Only a block from the Tuileries, so you can picnic in the garden if you like. This is a full-line shop, so you can get everything at one stop. They'll happily throw in free plastic knives and forks.

GARGANTUA
    284 Rue Saint-Honoré, 1er (Métro: Tuileries)

HÉDIARD
    Conveniently located around the bend from FAUCHON and MARQUISE DE SÉVIGNÉ (my favorite chocolate candies are bought here), Hédiard competes with the world-class food stores on its own. Hédiard has been in the food biz since the mid-1800s, and there is little you cannot buy in this shop. They will also deliver, but room service may not be amused.

HÉDIARD
    21 Place de la Madeleine, 8e (Métro: Madeleine)

LENOTRE

LeNotre will always mean chocolate and dessert to me but the store is a full-fledged *charcuterie*. You can get your picnic here, or your wedding party. They're open on Sunday (unusual) and will gladly guide you through any pig-out. For a price, they will deliver to your hotel.

LeNotre

44 Rue d'Auteuil, 16ᵉ (*Métro*: Michel-Ange Auteuil)

49 Avenue Victor Hugo, 16ᵉ (*Métro*: Victor Hugo)

5 Rue du Havre, 8ᵉ (*Métro*: Havre-Caumartin)

Chocolate

CHRISTIAN CONSTANT

The more things change, the more they become Constant, especially when you are considered one of the top chocolatiers in town. Open 8 A.M.–9 P.M.; also ice cream and other sweet treats.

Christian Constant

37 Rue d'Assas, 6ᵉ (*Métro*: Saint-Placide)

26 Rue du Bac, 6ᵉ (*Métro*: Rue du Bac)

LENOTRE

One of the older, more famous names in goo and goodies, LeNotre is known for chocolates, all desserts and their tearoom. A nice place to go for a gift for your hostess; Parisian prestige in a box. (See above for locations.)

LA MAISON DU CHOCOLAT

If you read American gourmet-food magazines, you'll find plenty of mentions of this boutique, which wraps its *chocolats* much as Hermès wraps its goodies. They are famous for their truffles, which are so rich you can't eat more than three a day (breakfast, lunch, dinner). Chocolates are handmade, a rarity these days, and mavens claim you can get no closer to heaven. This house got the highest rating in the French chocolate-tasting guidebook.

LA MAISON DU CHOCOLAT
8 Boulevard de la Madeleine, 9e (*Métro:* Madeleine)

MARQUISE DE SÉVIGNÉ
Since I like sweet chocolates, I send you here for the hazelnut candy that I discovered at the Hôtel Meurice and have been addicted to ever since. It has a picture of the Marquise herself on the golden foil. There are other divine chocolates here; I'm just addicted to this one flavor. There is also candy for diabetics. Those who prefer dark chocolates and more heady stuff may pooh pooh this as a source.

MARQUISE DE SÉVIGNÉ
32 Place de la Madeleine, 8e (*Métro:* Madeleine)

Books

To find English language books in Paris, you'll have to go to specialty stores and pay top dollar. While such stores are dotted all over Paris, there are two famous resources about a block apart.

GALIGNANI
Surrounded with handsome wood bookshelves, this old fashioned bookstore (yep, it's almost 200 years old) has editions in several languages and is headquarters for sophisticated travelers who are browsing and buying. Buy your TinTin here.

GALIGNANI
224 Rue de Rivoli no. 234, 1er (*Métro:* Tuileries)

W.H. SMITH
The English newsagent has a large shop in

Paris that's filled with everything, including a back wall jam-packed with American and British magazines. Buy British newspapers here, they are less expensive than American ones.

W.H. SMITH
248 Rue du Rivoli, 1er (*Métro*: Tuileries)

CHAPTER SEVEN

PARIS HOMESTYLE

French Style

Home may be anywhere I hang my hat, but if there's a little bit of French flavor, then I like my *chapeau* and my *château* all that much better. It's undeniable that French influence has touched all levels of home design, from the royalist to the pleasant peasant point of view. While Country French is considered a classic, my grandmother's idea of decorating had to do with draped silk swags, watered silk and reproduction Louis. Maybe she knew which Louis it was; surely I did not. Yet her Louis' remain even more classical than my Country French.

Those going to Paris can choose from either country or classical, or may want to latch onto the newer French designs—whether starkly modern from Philippe Starck or Shaker-*moderne* from Jacques Grange. For the first time in perhaps a hundred years, new home furnishings and decorating ideas are coming out of Paris. There are hot "new" French designers (led by Andrée Putman, who remains hot and new after about fifty years), and international eyes are looking to Paris for the latest definition of French style. Sure, the Disney people brought American architects to build the hotels at EuroDisney, but Americans are bringing French designers over here to design our hotels—and more.

True, Starck and Putman and maybe Grange (who has closed his New York retail shop) are the names you hear the most about, yet a browse through Paris' design showrooms, or even through *Vogue Decoration*, shows that the French have arrived.

Whether you choose French antiques, *brocante*, table linens or merely candles (wait till you see what the French can do with candles!), you're in for a treat. You need not do over the house or change your personal style, but please, make room for one lasting souvenir.

Booking French Style

Although there are several hardcover coffee-table books on French style currently available at your neighborhood bookstore, you'll also find a ton in French bookstores that you've never seen. These get pricey (very) and heavy. And you know I adore French newstands and kiosks. That's where I buy a few new magazines every day.

I always start with *Vogue Decoration* and *Elle Decoration*, two basics. *Marie Claire Maison* is less formal than *Elle Decor*, but jazzier than *Family Circle*, so it provides real-people design ideas and solutions. Truth be told, my fave is a magazine called *Maison & Travaux*, a do-it-yourself publication with such good picture instructions that you won't care that the text is in French.

Trouvailles is a magazine for antiques, arts and *brocante* with articles (in French) and plenty of ads and announcements about fairs and shows all over France. There are some listings for Belgium as well.

Smart Shopper's Homestyle

Let's face it, very few people with any smarts at all go to Paris to buy fine and formal antiques. Okay, maybe you're Lord Rothschild and you go to Paris for a few finishing touches for Spencer House. If you're playing in the big league, ignore this paragraph. There's no question that Paris has top of the line resources, but the truth is, if you have ever cast a wary eye at the bottom line, you know that Paris has top-of-the-line prices as well. Even Parisians leave town to buy antiques.

What people who have price in mind do is work the wide network of antiques shows, *brocante* fairs, auctions, flea markets and weekends in the country that provide not only wonderful entertainment, but far better prices than you'll ever find on the faubourg Saint-Honoré.

While Paris has very serious antiques, its joy— even for those who are shopping to be shipping— is really found in flea markets and alternative retail. Do note, however, that prices may be no lower than at big-time dealers—especially if you don't know what you are doing.

If you're a serious shopper and planning on doing some big-time buying, keep the following tips in mind:

- Buy from a reputable dealer with an international reputation.
- Prices are usually quoted in dollars once a price is over $5,000.
- There is no value-added tax on antiques.
- Make sure you are provided with the appropriate permissions and paperwork so that your purchase can leave the country. The French are not going to let any national treasures slip through their fingers.
- Insure for replacement value, not cost.

Decorator Showrooms

You are welcome to browse in decorator showrooms to get ideas and see what's new in gay Paree. Don't be surprised if many of the home furnishings fabrics suppliers want nothing to do with you unless you quickly brandish a business card that proves you are a designer. Most showrooms have U.S. representatives or distributors, and they do not want to undercut their own agents.

This leads to an even bigger point to bear in mind: you may find these same items are the same price (or even less) in the U.S.—especially if you have access to trade resources in the first place.

Mom, who ran a design firm in Manhattan, always traveled with business cards which she presented—not when browsing—but in final negotiations on price, or when the bill was presented. In flawless French she then asked for a 10% trade discount. It usually worked.

Also note that some fabrics and styles are British! They may look French and yummy and fabulous (and they are) but they are made in England! Buy them there, not in France, if you want to save.

Check out some of these showrooms to get a feel for the system:

MANUEL CANOVAS

Our living-room furniture is upholstered from Canovas, but I wasn't smart enough to buy it in Paris. While this showroom will not ship to you, you can take delivery in Paris (come back for your yardage in six to eight weeks). You can arrange for a shipper to take delivery if you want to take advantage of a magnificent 30% saving over U.S. prices. While Canovas is known as a fabric house, there are gift items and ceramics and candles and even bathing suits (for kids too) in the gift shop next door. This is the place to go for a fast injection of French style. The showroom is very much a trade kind of place; the gift shop should be on everyone's must-see list. Expect to pay dearly.

MANUEL CANOVAS
5–7 Place de Furstemberg, 6ᵉ (*Métro*: Saint-Germain-des-Prés)

JAC DEY

You can count on Jac Dey for really good fabrics for upholstery—choose traditional light geometrics, jacquards, florals, and French patterns. Although there is a Dey showroom at 979 Third Avenue in New York, the prices here are better—a good 20% below what similar goods would be if bought in the United States. But the cost of shipping probably would equal the *détaxe* discount.

JAC DEY

1 Rue de Furstemberg, 6e (*Métro*: Saint-Germain-des-Prés)

3 Rue Jacob, 6e (*Métro*: Saint-Germain-des-Prés)

ÉTAMINE

If all those French Laura Ashley shops didn't convince you that the French love the English country look, one minute inside Étamine will. This is a crowded, fabulous shop filled with papers and paints and stencil kits and veddy, veddy English everything. They are the agents for Colefax & Fowler, Collier & Campbell, Designer's Guild, Osborne & Little and Charles Hammond. Shipping is not possible.

ÉTAMINE

3 Rue Jacob, 6e (*Métro*: Saint-Germain-des-Prés)

PIERRE FREY

This is a boutique of fabrics, wall hangings, towels, bed quilts, luggage, purses, boxes and table linens in an explosion of paisleys that is reminiscent of India, yet very French all at the same time. I consider this look as fancy country French formal if you can imagine such a thing: it's sold at Bergdorf Goodman. Try the scented candle.

PIERRE FREY

2 Rue de Furstemberg, 6e (*Métro*: Saint-Germain-des-Prés)

47 Rue des Petits-Champs, 1er (*Métro*: Palais-Royal)

48 Rue Saint-Dominique, 7e (*Métro*: Invalides)

NOBILIS

A classic-looking traditional showroom, Nobilis is one of those airy, modern spaces that could be anywhere in the world, selling what it sells best. There are pads of paper and pencils, boards of fabrics and wallpapers—it's all just as you know it—but it's open to the public and is in the best location in Paris, right behind the church of Saint-Germain-des-Prés. In short, you do not have to be a decorator to buy. The fabrics are gorgeous, running from the palest of pastel cottons to the most brilliant silk moirés. There is furniture just down the street—another good source. Shipping is no problem.

NOBILIS

29 and 38 Rue Bonaparte, 6e (*Métro*: Saint-Germain-des-Prés-des-Prés)

ZUMSTEG

Although there really is a Mr. Zumsteg, the name refers to the fabric house that became famous when Yves Saint-Laurent revealed that he chose many of his fabrics here. There also is a Zumsteg interiors line, which comes from the main offices in Zurich, but which can be bought in Paris for much less than in the United States. Most of the fabrics are extremely expensive and sophisticated. Those in the know, know.

ZUMSTEG

4 Rue de Furstemberg, 6e (*Métro*: Saint-Germain-des-Prés)

Big Names in Homestyle

CRISTAL LALIQUE

One glance at Lalique's crystal door and there's no doubt that you've entered one of the wonders of the world. Get a look at the Lalique-designed Olympic medals created for the 1992 Winter Games. René Lalique began work as a silversmith, but switched to jewelry-making in 1894. One of his first customers was Sarah Bernhardt, who adored his crystal hair combs, and, as they say in clichés, the rest is history. Today Cristal Lalique is sold in 110 countries. The Rue Royale headquarters is sort of like a museum: people come to stare more than they shop. The prices are the same as at factory sources on the Rue de Paradis, by the way, so don't think you may beat the tags here. Besides, you get *détaxe*, and everyone is friendly, speaks English, and ships to the United States.

CHRISTAL LALIQUE

11 Rue Royale, 8ᵉ (*Métro*: Concorde)

PIERRE DEUX/SOULEIADO

You have to be a real Pierre Deux freak to know that Charles Demery is the man who designs all those Provençal prints you adore or to know that Pierre Deux is the name of the American franchise for those prints but *is not* the name of the company in Europe. So remember the name Souleiado—which will get you happily through France.

There are thirty-seven Souleiados in France alone (nineteen U.S. Pierre Deux; three shops in Tokyo) and three Souleiado shops in Paris—although I hate to tell you about the one in the FORUM DES HALLES, because it pales compared to the Left Bank flagship. The Rue de Seine shop, the *great* shop, is everything it should be. You will be in Country French heaven. Be sure to see all parts of the shop (there are two separate rooms); the main shop winds around a bit to what looks like another showroom in the far back, where more fabrics are sold by the meter. There is a showroom for the trade next door.

I asked Souleiado to ship; they immediately

responded that they certainly would not—if I wanted to buy in the United States I should go to a Pierre Deux shop!

What I didn't tell them is that Pierre Deux goods can be cheaper in the U.S., if you wait for one of their twice-a-year sales. There are sometimes warehouse sales in Mamaroneck, NY (watch for an ad in the New York Times), but each local boutique has a sale when cotton prints are sold for as little as $8 a yard. Save your francs for something else. But stop by to visit, to get decorating ideas, to know you really are in Paris.

SOULEIADO

78 Rue de Seine, 6e (Métro: Mabillon)
Forum des Halles, 1er (Métro: Châtelet)
85 Avenue Paul-Doumer, 16e (Métro: Muette)

D. PORTHAULT

Porthault was making fancy bed linens with pretty colored flowers on them long before the real world was ready for patterned sheets or the notion that a person could spend $1,000 on their bedclothes and still be able to sleep at night.

There are two Porthault lines of goods for sale in America: One is identical to what you buy in France, and just costs more in the United States; the other is contracted by the Porthault family and is available only in the United States. Porthault has released one fabric design a year to an American sheet company (both Dan River and Wamsutta have had the honor) for sheets that look, but do not feel like their French counterparts. French Porthault is only percale or voile, with some tablecloths done in linen, but with less and less linen being made. There is also no fitted sheet in the French line (you can have one custom-made for extra money).

The French laminated products are not sold in the United States; the American wallpaper is not sold in France. One Porthault saleswoman swore that our pattern was not "theirs" because she was unfamiliar with the American wallpapers. The Montaigne shop does have a whopper of a sale in January, during which they unload everything at half the retail price, or less! You cannot phone in orders from the United States.

You may think that Porthault is totally beyond you and hurry by to avoid temptation; I beg you to reconsider. There are many little accessories and gift items that are affordable, fun and speak volumes when presented. I always travel with my Porthault shower cap ($20) because it makes me smile and beats those plastic jobs supplied by hotels. I gave my niece a traditional Porthault bib when she was born: $25. You have to know what Porthault means in order to appreciate items like this, but for those in the know, this could be your gift headquarters. They wrap.

D. PORTHAULT

18 Avenue Montaigne, 8ᵉ (*Métro:* Alma Marceau)

Tabletop and Gifts

AU BAIN MARIE

This is one of my favorites stores in Paris; the ultimate "kitchen" shop for foodies, good cooks and stylists who love to set a pretty table. In fact, even if you hate to cook, but like to look at pretty things for the home and table, this is a must. You'll find antique linens, faience and colored mother-of-pearl table settings that they sell in Barneys in New York for a lot more money. This street is right off the faubourg; the store is very convenient—there's no excuse to pass this one by.

AU BAIN MARIE

10–12 Rue Boissy-d'Anglas, 8ᵉ (*Métro:* Concorde)

AUX DECORS DE MARTRES

An art workshop where repro faience is made in the old country style; styles are hand-painted in the tradition of the 18th century. On the Ile de la Cité, which adds to the charm. Worth tracking down for a look, even if you don't buy.

AUX DECORS DE MARTRES
1 Quai Aux Fleurs, 4e (Métro: Hôtel de Ville)

AUX ÉTATS-UNIS

This has nothing to do with shopping in the U.S. or with American-made products for that matter, despite the store name. This esoteric little shop is mostly a luggage store, but they also sell travel gadgets and have a specialty in leather-goods and porcelain dishes for dogs. Since treating the dog as if he were a member of the family (he is, he is) is a French tradition, you may want to see this rather unique pet selection—and pick up a souvenir dish for *le chien*...or *le chat*.

AUX ÉTATS-UNIS
229 Rue Saint-Honoré, 1er (Métro: Concorde or Tuileries)

GALERIE ARCHITECTURE MINATURE

I don't happen to be a big fan of those little clay houses and village pieces that make up the Gault collection, but many visitors think they make a nice souvenir or decorative touch. Don't expect the houses to be inexpensive, but they do cost less than in the U.S. It'll take about $100 to start building your own village.

GALERIE ARCHITECTURE MINATURE
206 Rue de Rivoli, 1er (Métro: Tuileries)

GENEVIEVE LETHU

This designer has a boutique in PRINTEMPS MAISON, or you can check out any of her several freestanding stores in Paris. She does what I consider some of the most refreshing tabletop in

Paris: color is bold and extravagant, prints are exotic without being beyond the fringe. The elegance mixes with both contemporary tabletop and country looks—even a formal setting will work. Tablecloths are my favorite, but there's all sorts of tabletop design as well as yardgoods.

GENEVIEVE LETHU

95 Rue de Rennes, 6e (Métro: Saint-Germain-des-Prés)

LA DAME BLANCHE

Nestled in with the TT's right on the Rue de Rivoli, this teensy-tiny shop sells reproduction faience as well as Limoges boxes and Louis-style porcelains.

LA DAME BLANCHE

186 Rue de Rivoli, 1er (Métro: Tuileries)

LAURE JAPY

One glance at the windows of this tony 7e shop and you'll know why so many designers feel the need to walk the Paris streets: there's more ideas and inspiration here than you can get in a week in your hometown mall. After you've memorized the windows, get a load of the insides where dishes, table linens, place settings and more are all done up with Parisian chic.

LAURE JAPY

34 Rue du Bac, 7e (Métro: Rue du Bac)

MARECHAL

This looks like a perfume TT from the street and not a memorable one at that. Still, there's a reason to stop in. Trust me...downstairs there's a great selection of Limoges boxes. Ignore the fragrance. Check out their catalogue, which gurantees the French bargain price and includes mailing to the U.S.

MARECHALE

232 Rue de Rivoli, 1er (Métro: Concorde or Tuileries)

PORTO SANTO

If you are into the country look and don't care about the country of origin, these Portuguese-made goods will blend well with French and American country style. Many of the items are carried in the U.S.; you may find no savings. Since the shop is right off the Rue Saint-Honoré on your way to the Hotel Meurice, you can at least pop in for an eyeful of style. Some linens but mostly dishes and glassware.

PORTO SANTO
7 Rue du 29 Julliet, 1er (Métro: Tuileries)

Kitchen Style

Paris is rightfully renowned for its table arts; luckily for tourists there are a number of kitchen supply houses within a block or two of each other, so you can see a lot without going out of your way. Price is not the object here; selection is everything.

LA CORPO

This one isn't my favorite, but they too have a selection of kitchenwares including much equipment. While you may be tempted, remember that electric gadgets are a no-no. Still, there's lot of pots and pans and supplies that are very enticing.

LA CORPO
19 Rue Montmartre, 1er (Métro: Étienne-Marcel or Les Halles)

DUTHILLEUL & MINART

This shop sells professional clothing for chefs, kitchen staff, waiters, etc. It would be a great resource for creative fashion freaks or teens. You can buy anything from kitchen clogs to aprons; a toque costs $12 while the *veste chef* is $30. There are various styles of aprons (make good gifts) and many wine supplies or wine-related items.

DUTHILLEUL & MINART
14 Rue de Turbigo, 1er (*Métro*: Étienne-Marcel)

MORA

Similar to A. SIMON but with more utensils (over 5,000 in stock); it also has a salon for bakery goods that sells *fèves* in small (and large) packages.

MORA
13 Rue Montmartre, 1er (*Métro*: Étienne-Marcel)

A. SIMON

A major supplier of kitchen and cooking supplies for over one hundred years, this store is conveniently located down the street from the YSL outlet. You can buy everything from dishes to menus here; I buy white paper doilies by the gross—they have many sizes and shapes not available in the U.S.—at fair prices. Touch everything; this is a wonderland of gadgets and goodies. Remember, Rue Montmartre is not in Montmartre; it is near FORUM DES HALLES.

A. SIMON
38 Rue Montmartre, 2e (*Métro*: Étienne-Marcel)

Logo Style

Combine the notion of a souvenir with chic and you have something from a famous French address. I once stole an ashtray from the restaurant in the Eiffel Tower (I was seventeen, give me a break); I still collect sugar cubes from the CAFÉ DE LA PAIX. If you're willing to put your money where you hand is, there are several shops selling logo merchandise.

BOUTIQUE CRILLON

The Crillon is one of the most famous hotels in Paris. Even if you aren't staying there, you may want to go for tea. Or to shop. They have two boutiques: one in the hotel and one in the real world. The merchandise is a rich blend of bathrobes, terry slippers, dishes, handbags and about every other life-style item you could imagine. Some is decorated with the hotel crest; much is just beautiful to look at. Prices begin around $30.

BOUTIQUE CRILLON

Crillon Hotel, 10 Place de la Concorde, 8e (*Métro*: Concorde)

17 Rue de la Paix, 2e (*Métro*: Tuileries or Opéra)

BOUTIQUE DU CAFÉ FLORE

The CAFÉ FLORE is one of the three famous Paris bistros grouped together on the Left Bank (the other two are DEUX MAGOTS and LIPP), but so far it's the only one to have opened its own shop. The tiny store is around the corner from the café and is just adorable. You get a free chocolate when you wander in (you may buy a box) and can choose from dishes, serving pieces, papergoods and all sorts of gift items. It's quite classy and not the least bit tacky. Great gifts and souvenirs for the Hemingway freaks and those in the know.

BOUTIQUE DU CAFÉ FLORE

26 Rue Saint-Benoît, 6e (*Métro*: Saint Germain-des-Prés)

COMPTIOR DE LA TOUR D'ARGENT

La Tour D'Argent is one of the most famous restaurants in Paris and has withstood the comings and goings of new rivals. Whether you eat there or not, you may want to shop next door where you can get a picnic, foodstuffs to go, in gift formats, etc. There's also ashtrays, crystal, china, etc. If you eat at Maxim's, they give you the ashtray as a souvenir. At Tour D'Argent, you buy your own.

COMPTIOR DE LA TOUR D'ARGENT

2 Rue du Cardinal Lemoine, 5e (*Métro*: Maubert-Mutualité)

China, Crystal and Silver

BACCARAT

Baccarat has two headquarters—the factory in Paris, which has a museum and a gigantic shop (no seconds, sorry) and the boutique in the high-rent district—prices are the same at either venue.

Entering the main Baccarat showroom in search of the shop is confusing the first time, since you must walk through the company's offices and head up some stairs. Once up the stairs the museum sprawls in front of you; the shop is to your left. It's hard to tell one from the other.

There are long, long tables laid out with merchandise in rows (in both shop and museum)—you may touch. You can even try on the earrings. Whether or not you can walk out with your choice is up to the gods. Baccarat is often six to seven months behind in its orders, so if they don't have what you want in the shop, they will send it to you...someday. Prices are not negotiable. They ship anywhere in the world and will mail-order. If there is breakage in your package, Baccarat will replace the item—but of course. The selection is not as overwhelming on the Rue Royale, and although the location is more sublime you won't have as much fun.

BACCARAT

30 bis Rue de Paradis, 10ᵉ (Métro: Château d'Eau)

11 Place de la Madeleine, 8ᵉ (Métro: Concorde)

BERNARDAUD

If you're making the rounds of the hoity-toity tabletop houses that are undeniably French (and swank), don't miss Bernardaud, which means Limoges china. Especially impressive are the newer contemporary designs, with their Art Deco roots. If you don't have to ship, you can save over New York prices.

BERNARDAUD
11 Rue Royale, 8e (Métro: Concorde)

DAUM
While you may think of Daum and their large-size lead crystal cars, think twice now that they have this two-level shop and can display a lot of inventive glass art and colored-glass pieces that will surely become collector's items.

DAUM
4 Rue de la Paix, 2e (Métro: Opéra)

PUIFORCAT
If you believe in studying only the best, here's a place where you can get your graduate degree in fine French silver. Founded in 1820 and dedicated since that date to making shoppers swoon, the most collectible pieces are currently from the late 1920s and '30s.

PUIFORCAT
2 Avenue Montaigne, 8e (Métro: Alma Marceau)

Paradise and More

The main street for wholesale crystal, china and tabletop is the Rue de Paradis, where headquarters for many big names are located. There's just a few catches: this is a low-rent district, but prices here are no different than in high-rent districts. It's a bit of a walk from the *métro* stop in a not-so-interesting area (but it's not dangerous), or a $8 taxi ride from the 1er. It's fun, true, but you might prefer a quick visit to CRISTAL VENDÔME which is back in the main shopping district.

If you head for Rue de Paradis, be sure to take in the Baccarat museum. Then just browse from one shop to the next. Prices are generally fixed by the factories; there is little negotiation. After a few shops, they'll all look alike to you. Many of the stores carry other European brands; all have bridal registry.

CRISTAL VENDÔME

Right underneath good old Hotel Intercontinental on Rue Castiglione you can find a factory-direct store that will even ship to the U.S. (You can phone in an order once you have bought in person, which is a service factories will not offer.) Various lines are sold here, which makes the shopping easy: Baccarat, Lalique, Daum, etc. The store offers tax-free prices, which means they are the same as at the airport. I priced a Lalique necklace and found it to be $200 (almost half price) less than in the U.S.

CRISTAL VENDÔME
1 Rue de Castiglione, 1er (*Métro*: Concorde)

ÉDITIONS PARADIS

Enormous source with so much stuff that you'll be nervous if you are carrying a big floppy handbag. Fancy and done up with table settings, this one carries the small Limoges boxes that make such perfect collectibles.

ÉDITIONS PARADIS
29 Rue de Paradis, 10e (*Métro*: Château d'Eau)

LA TISANIERE PARADIS

A country-style resource on a street filled with more traditional showrooms, this porcelain shop has stacks of kitchenwares and tabletop at prices that are fair. Some promotional items are downright cheap. Much fun.

LA TISANIERE PARADIS
21 Rue de Paradis, 10e (*Métro*: Château d'Eau)

LIMOGES-UNIC

Despite the sound of the name of this factory, don't think they sell only Limoges or that the place is unique. It's merely one of the bigger, better stocked traditional stores on the Rue de Paradis. Locals consider this the anchor of the neighborhood, although there are other similar shops. They will ship; *détaxe*, of course.

LIMOGES-UNIC

   58 Rue de Paradis, 10ᵉ (*Métro*: Château d'Eau)

GEO MARTEL

   Another breath of fresh air for those who easily get bored with the mostly traditional and all-too-perfect stores that line the street—this store is small and specializes in faience. All the styles are reproductions of 300-year-old patterns.

GEO MARTEL

   2 Rue de Paradis, 10ᵉ (*Métro*: Château d'Eau)

PORCELAINOR

   Despite the name, they don't just sell porcelain, this is headquarters for Christofle, and just about everything else too.

PORCELAINOR

   31 Rue de Paradis, 10ᵉ (*Métro*: Château d'Eau)

Fabrics

MADURA

   Offering what they call a "system," Madura is a rather large chain of fabric stores selling precut and finished fabrics for draping over furniture. Their patterns are copies of the popular prints of the day, and for about $50 you can find something very interesting—this is an especially good source for those with summer homes that may need some sprucing up, or those who are first starting out with apartments and homes and have no budget for re-upholstering their tag-sale finds.

MADURA

   66 Rue de Rennes, 6ᵉ (*Métro*: Saint-Germain-des-Prés)

LES OLIVADES

   I have been told that Les Olivades was started in the mid-1970s when someone in the SOULEIADO hierarchy departed and started a new firm. Indeed, Les Olivades reminds me of the

Pierre Deux/Souleiado look, although the colors are more muted and pastel. The firm specializes in the same type of merchandise so that you can buy fabric by the yard, placemats, tablecloths, napkins and tabletop or umbrellas, gifts, items for travel or the handbag, etc. While the goods are not cheap, they are about 30% less expensive than Souleiado, right there in France. The store is small and a little hard to find—it's on a small street directly behind the Place de Passy. The yardgoods are less expensive than Souleiado.

LES OLIVADES
25 Rue de l'Annonciation, 16e (Métro: Muette)

Antiques

One of the pleasures of browsing in Paris is the wide array of antiques shops and the general assumption that Paris is one of the world capitals for antiques. Whether you're buying real antiques or just some "old stuff", remember that the U.S. Customs people define an antique as something that is at least 100 years old. If the piece does not come with paperwork, you must have a receipt or bill of lading from the dealer that says what the piece is and its origin and age. The French are getting more and more sticky about what can be taken out of the country; they are even trying to keep *fripes* and important items of costume in the country now.

The expensive, museum-quality antiques are pretty much gathered in the tony little shops along the Rue du faubourg-Saint-Honoré; DIDIER AARON, which has a major reputation, is in the 16e. While you're doing the faubourg you can see enough hoity-toity dealers to get the drift of what the high-end antiques scene is in Paris. There has been a lot of movement on the street due to the recession, but you can pop into these or other shops just to get the notion. You are wearing

Chanel, aren't you? If you are a big spender and want to go to Didier Aaron it is worth the taxi fare. Besides, if you have this much money, you probably brought your car and driver with you anyway, so what's one more stop?

Mid-priced antiques are scattered about town in various pockets of pleasure: the Left Bank; the *villages*; and the markets of Saint-Ouen.

You'll come across shops scattered everywhere around the city—but these are the main areas. Unless you collect a certain something, you'll probably have more fun if you roam around these areas and wander into any of the shops that may interest you, rather than seeking out one address. If you just want to browse and get the feel of the antiques scene without doing anything as formal as the Faubourg, get over to the Left Bank. The shops with addresses on Boulevard Saint-Germain-des-Prés may be a tad more expensive than the others, because they are paying higher rent. The best stuff is nestled behind the church. (See page 79.) If you head out on your own, just weave from one charming shop to the next. Don't miss the cute little Rue de Furstemberg, which is so tiny it could be passed over with a sneeze. The Rue Jacob and Rue de Seine area is the heart of the browse, but don't forget to fan all the way to the river where the fancier shops reign over the quai.

Many neighborhood shops belong to an association called *Association des Antiquaires et Galeries d'Art du Carré Rive Gauche*. Ask about it at your favorite Left Bank antiques shop. Each of the 120 different member shops contribute one gleaming item to make up a show. On opening night musicians in costume stroll the streets, and everyone has an exceptionally good time.

There is a printed brochure that lists everyone's name and address; simply phone and ask them to send you one.

If you can't get to all 120 shops, here's my ranking of the best of the bunch, in order of personal preference, made as a serious shopper. If you're just looking, any old place will offer charm and selection.

The Villages

A *village* in Paris (say vil-ahge) is not a subdivision of an *arrondissement*, but a place for good antiques. The *villages* are the buildings that house many antiques dealers under one roof. If you need a rainy-day-in-Paris occupation, a trip to any *village* probably will do it; some are open on Sunday for your shopping pleasure.

VILLAGE SAINT-PAUL

This can be a little hard to find if you aren't patient, since it's hidden in a medieval warren of streets and there are dealers on the streets as well as in a specific building. This is a block or so of antiques dealers crammed into a small space between the Seine and the church of Saint-Paul, very close to the Marais and to the Bastille. The *village* niche is between the Rue Saint-Paul, the Rue Charles V, the Rue des Jardins-Saint-Paul and the Rue de l'Ave-Maria.

Get off the *métro* at Saint-Paul and walk toward the river. Or walk along the quai going toward Bastille and hang a left when you spy your first antiques shop on the corner of the Rue Saint-Paul. Hours are generally Thursday–Monday, 11 A.M.–7 P.M. There are many shops to visit. Prices can be steep, but the variety of the merchandise, combined with the charm of the neighborhood, makes this a delightful way to pass the time. A good stop to piggyback with your visit to the Marais.

VILLAGE SAINT-PAUL
Rue Saint-Paul, 4e (*Métro*: Saint-Paul)

LE LOUVRE DES ANTIQUAIRES

This is like a department store of some 250 dealers. It's questionable if you'll have more fun here or across the street at the culture palace. You can at least shop here. Many mavens claim this is the single best one-stop source in Paris because quality is high, dealers have reputations to protect, there's a little bit of bargaining and enough affordable small pieces to feel some sense of triumph and you haven't pounded the pavement going from shop to shop. Indoors is a restaurant, a shipping agent and everything you'll need to make your stay here complete.

LE LOUVRE DES ANTIQUAIRES

2 Place du Palais-Royal, 1er (*Métro*: Palais-Royal)

LE VILLAGE SUISSE

No gnomes here hammering at little pieces of chocolate or making watches; just a lot of dealers in the mid-to-high-priced range, with some very respectable offerings. There are 150 shops in an area one block long and two blocks wide. The Village Suisse is near the Eiffel Tower and l'École Militaire, but don't be getting your hopes up for cute or quaint—it's just two sets of modern buildings and one old one. Part of it was originally created for a world's fair. Prices are not outrageous, and most stores offer shipping.

LE VILLAGE SUISSE

54 Avenue de la Motte-Picquet, 15e (*Métro*: La Motte-Picquet)

AU BON MARCHÉ

Au Bon Marché is indeed a department store, and there are antiques in both parts of the store. On the second floor of Magasin 1 is the plebeian section, used goodies that are quite affordable; the location is poor: in the middle of the furniture section, so you may have trouble locating the area. In Magasin 2, walk in toward the grocery store and take the escalator on the right to the first floor, which is a flea market of antiques dealers. Each boutique is separately owned. You can find many good buys for under $100 in the approximately thirty-five stalls here. You get the feeling of a flea market without having to go far to find one or without the overwhelming feeling of endless stalls.

AU BON MARCHÉ
38 Rue de Sèvres, 6e (*Métro*: Sèvres-Babylone)

The *Brocante* Shows

Sadema is an organization which hosts *brocante* shows. These are annual events, most frequently held at the same time and place each year. They are announced in the papers or you can call, write, or fax for their schedule: Sadema, Tolbiac-Messena, 25 Quai de la Gare, Ce 18, Paris 75644; phone 45-85-01-85; fax 45-85-22-66. Some shows are weekend events; other last for up to a fortnight. Sadema charges admission of $5–$6 per person.

Ferraille de Paris: Held in the Parc Floral de Paris (Bois de Vincennes), this fair is toward the end of February every year. (*Métro*: Porte Dorée)

Brocante de Printemps: A March event that usually lasts ten days; heralds the coming of spring, of course. (*Métro*: Edgar Quinet)

Brocante de Bastille: Held on both sides of the canal; pay near the Place de la Bastille; there are bridges to the other side. Usually held for ten days in April, this is particularly nice when the weather is good. (*Métro*: Bastille)

Brocante de Paris: This is a huge event is the talk of the town and those who hope to get a designer bargain. Ten days in May. (*Métro*: Brochant)

The Markets of Saint-Ouen

Also known simply as the Marché aux Puces, or the famous Flea Market, Saint-Ouen comprises several different markets, each with its own kind of dealers and each with its own special feel. While there are other things to buy out here besides home decor, I have listed this detailed account of the markets here, rather than in the general flea market section, because the predominant concern for most shoppers will be decorative. See page 116 for a list of other flea markets; the one at Vanves does not feature furniture but does have many tabletop items.

The Saint-Ouen markets have grown up on a series of little streets and alleys; and now comprises over 75 acres of flea market sprawling through this suburb. The market most frequently bears the name of the street on which it rests—even though you may be hard-pressed to find the original street sign. The markets themselves are usually well marked.

Usually the stalls open onto the street or a walkway but have some covered parts; these are not street vendors set up garage-sale style. Even the informal markets are sheltered. There is some amount of street action and selling off makeshift tables, but not a lot.

There is, however, plenty of street action in terms of stalls, candy stands, blue jeans dealers and what-not as you walk from the *métro* to the flea market. This is not the flea market you are looking for; these dealers should all be ignored.

Do remember there are plenty of places to eat on the premises, not as many places to go to the bathroom as you might like and more pickpockets and rowdy boys than the French government would like to admit.

If you feel like you need to have a system for working this vast amount of space, try mine. Start with the big guns (Biron, Cambon) and the markets in that area and walk your way back so that Malik becomes one of your last stops. In fact, if you like Marché Malik as little as I do, you'll be happy to run out of there and call it a day.

To do it my way, you'll turn into the market streets on the Rue des Rosiers (if your back is to the *métro* station from where you came, you'll turn left); you'll work this street till the good stuff peters out and cut to the left by shopping your way through the Marché Paul Bert. Then you'll go right on the Rue Vallès until you've shopped it and then retrace your steps cutting through Malassis and right on out of there.

Note that there are freestanding antiques stores as well as the big (and small) markets. (*Métro*: Porte de Clignancourt)

Marché Antica: Just a little-bitty building refinished in the Memphis Milano teal-blue-and-*crème* look. This market is filled with cute shops selling small collectibles of good quality at pretty good prices.

Marché Biron: This is the single fanciest market in the place; it's one of the first markets you'll come to on Rue des Rosiers but not the first. This should be the first stop for dealers who are looking for serious stuff.

Marché Cambon: Another serious market but a little less refined—the dealers are usually busy hobnobbing with each other and may ignore you totally. You'll see furnishings in various states of refinish and find dealers in various states of mind—some know what they have and are very hard-nosed about it; others want to move out the merchandise and will deal with you. They are particularly responsive to genuine dealers who know their stuff and speak some French. The selection is less formal and more eclectic than at Biron; there are rows of stalls along lanes or aisles.

Marché Dauphine: Newer village of some 300

shops opposite the Marché Vernaison on the Rue des Rosiers, making it one of the first places you want to hit when you get to the market area. It's enclosed with a balcony and factory-like high-tech atmosphere under glass rooftop and industrial lighting. There is a shipping agency on hand.

Marché des Rosiers: A very small market specializing in the period between 1900 and 1930. There are about thirteen small stalls in an enclosed building in a U-shape.

Marché Jules Valles: I like this one although it's small and junky; it's got reproduction brass items for the home mixed in with real antiques and real repro everything else. Outside the door is a dealer who just sells Suze collectibles. I collect 'em, natch.

Marché Malik: Ugh! It may be famous for its *fripes*—used clothes—but I find it seedy, disgusting, expensive and dangerous. Need I say more?

Marché Paul Bert: Are we having fun yet? This is the market that is more outdoorsy than the rest; it surrounds the Marché Serpette in three alleys forming a U. This market is both outside and inside, with lower-end merchandise, including Art Deco, *moderne*, and country furniture. Most of the items here have not been repaired or refinished. There could be some great buys here, but you need to have a good eye and to know your stuff. Piles of suitcases, carts, dolls and buttons in bins. Yummy.

Marché Serpette: This market is in a real building, not a Quonset hut. There is carpet on the floor, and each vendor has a stall number and a closing metal door. There also are nice, clean bathrooms on the second floor.

Marché Vernaison: I like this market a lot, although the new building puts me off a bit. There isn't that much I want to buy, I just like to prowl the various teeny showrooms. There are a few fabrics, textiles, trim and needleworks mavens here who always have things I covet.

Auctions in Paris

HÔTEL DROUOT

If you prefer your used furniture to come by way of an auction house, Marie Jo swears this is the place for a serious deal. In Paris the auction business is tightly controlled and one house—the Hôtel Drouot—has all the business.

You can buy their magazine on newsstands and get an instant look at the action for the month.

Some ninety auctioneers are in the main house and several auctions will go on simultaneously. The ninety auctioneers are all shareholders—equal partners—in the business, and in that sense the place is run much like a law firm. Speaking of lawyers, there are lawyers in France who specialize in auctions, because this is a very, very different business from the one you know and love in the United States and the United Kingdom.

Auctions are held every day except in summer, when they are not held on weekends. They always begin at 2 P.M. and go until concluded, usually about 6:30 P.M. Previews are on Wednesday until 11 A.M.

Drouot is a weird and fascinating place. At the entrance, an information counter has catalogues and notices of future sales. Three TV sets on the ground floor show different parts of the building, and there is an appraiser who—free of charge—will tell you if an item you bring in is worthy of auction, and then will appraise it for you. The estimate is done in a small, private room. If you agree with the estimate, you can set a date for your auction. The seller pays an 8% to 10% commission to the house.

The auction rooms are of various sizes; some can be divided or opened according to need. All the rooms are carpeted; art and/or tapestries are on the walls. The clients sit on chairs to watch the bidding; paddles are not used. Most of the clients are dealers; we have never noticed a very jazzy crowd here, even when we went to a Goya auction. All business is in French; if you are not fluent, please bring your own translator or expert, or book a translator ahead of time. (Call 42-46-17-11 to arrange for a translator.)

You needn't register to bid; anyone can walk in, sit down and bid. You can pay in cash up to 10,000 francs. French people may write local checks; Americans cannot write checks. If you have only American money with you, there is a change bureau in the house. If you pay in cash, you can walk out with your item. Shills are occasionally used by some dealers to drive up the price. Auctioneers are familiar with all the dealers and could possibly choose to throw a piece their way; the dealers may pool on an item. It's a dirty little business out there in the big, bad world.

You are responsible for shipping; there is no shipping office in the auction house. You start paying storage charges after twenty-four hours.

All auctions have catalogues, and the lots are numbered and defined in the catalogue. You do not need a catalogue to enter a preview or an auction, as you do in New York. The conditions of the sale are plainly printed inside the first page of the catalogue (in French only).

Changing times and preparation for the unification of Europe have forced France—especially Paris—to change its auction techniques in order to compete with the rest of Europe. In the old system, an estate was auctioned off in a big chunk—the whole thing—so that anything and everything would come up for sale. Nowadays, you still have estates sold as one big lump at the Hôtel Drouot, but you also have the categorical auctions that are popular in Britain and in the U.S., which France never had before—important paintings taken from various estates and saved for a big sale, for example. When an entire estate is auctioned off there is usually nothing "important" (as the dealers tend to say) for sale. Important works are now being saved for major auctions. Such big-time auctions are held in the relatively new Hôtel Drouot, which is actually in renovated digs, since the auction house took over an existing theater on none other than the prestigious Avenue Montaigne.

When you read auction catalogues in Paris, note that Hôtel Drouot listings with an "R" after them (for Richelieu) refer to the old location, and an "M" refers to the Avenue Montaigne location.

HÔTEL DROUOT

9 Rue Drouot, 9e (*Métro*: Le Peletier)

15 Avenue Montaigne, 8e (*Métro*: Alma Marceau)

CHAPTER EIGHT

PARIS TOURS AND DAY TRIPS

Tour 1: All-Day-Designer-See-It-All Tour

This tour gives you a good workout while you see a lot of the best shopping in Paris, but not necessarily the best prices. If you are mostly window shopping, you can speed this tour up to half a day.

1) Begin the tour at PRINTEMPS MAISON on Boulevard Haussmann. They open at 9:35 A.M.—if you are the on-time sort. Remember to save your purchase receipts for *détaxe* at the end of the shopping tour. Don't mind the perfume and makeup on the street level, take the escalator up. Get a free spritz on the way. Take in three floors of housewares; ignore the non-French merchandise, of which there can be much.

2) Now for GALERIES LAFAYETTE, main store please. Check out the stained glass ceiling, the souvenirs (why not?), the toy department and of course, the designer floors. You might want to take notes on the new styles and trends.

3) The next three stops should be chosen according to your personal interest: MONO-PRIX, a dime store; LAFAYETTE GOURMET, a super supermarket; and BOUCHARA, a fabric store that sells materials similar to the latest designer prints, home furnishings fabrics and more. All of these are on the Boulevard Haussmann. You can pass them by and hit

Rue Tronchet and walk toward the Seine; you are headed toward Place de la Madeleine. This is all of one block. There are a number of fancy food shops around here; surely you have time to press your nose to the glass at FAUCHON (#26 Place de la Madeleine). If it's lunch time, or even a little before (beat the crowds), try the famous tearoom LADURÉE which is on the Rue Royale, which is the name of the Rue Tronchet after you pass the Madeleine. Ladurée looks like the kind of tearoom your grandmother would take you to; they have desserts galore but also salads, omelettes and moderate prices—plus a great- looking clientele.

4) From there, continue up Rue Royale, where you won't want to miss anything, especially LALIQUE (#11) and the other fine and fancy showrooms for dishes and silverware, even Swatch watches. The best of the block is the duty free shop PARFUMERIE CHAMPS-ÉLYSÉES (#8) which gives a flat 30% discount on everything you buy—no limits, no mess with *détaxe*.

5) Now head away from the Place de la Concorde to the Rue du faubourg-Saint-Honoré, where you should turn left. This is one of the swankiest streets in Paris; you will want to window shop if nothing more. Be sure to see the door with the ocean in it at CARITA (#11) and everything that's inside HERMÈS. About two blocks past the Élysée Palace, turn left on Avenue Matignon and proceed to ANNA LOWE (#55), where big-name clothes (Chanel, etc.) from last season are sold at discount. Follow Avenue Matignon to the Champs-Élysées, strolling on this famous street (toward the Arc de Triomphe) to your heart's content. I don't happen to like this famous street very much, so I hit the VIRGIN MEGASTORE and PRISUNIC and then cross

the murderous traffic and walk toward Rond Point where the Champs-Élysées meets the Avenue Montaigne. Turn right onto the Avenue Montaigne and put on your sunglasses. Otherwise you might be blinded by the light.

6) Stroll the entire length of the Avenue Montaigne which is only two or three blocks—I like the side of the street away from the Arc de Triomphe, since it has more shops. But there are plenty of good shops and you should probably plan on prowling both sides of this street—working you way up and then down again. Don't miss INES DE LA FRESSANGE, LACROIX, PORTHAULT, etc. When you get to the end you have choices: double back and hit the other side of the street so you end up back at Rond Point; follow the signs to *bateaux-mouche* and collapse on a boat tour of Paris; or hop in the *métro* at Alma Marceau, conveniently located right at the end of Avenue Montaigne.

7) You've chosen the other side of the street (smart move); don't forget that at NINA RICCI there is a bargain basement in couture gowns downstairs.

8) After shopping your heart out, and absorbing so much visual splendor, take a peaceful walk through the green paths that lead toward the American Embassy and the Place de la Concorde. Now you get your just reward for not buying too much: tea at the Hotel Crillon. Don't forget they have a hotel gift shop—selling just Crillon name brand merchandise—right by the front door. Now's the time to buy yourself a bathrobe and some slippers. If the Crillon and a hoity-toity tea are not what you have in mind and funky is more your style, walk past the Crillion and continue on the Rue de Rivoli until you get to ANGELINA (#226) beneath the Hôtel

Meurice. Here you can have a less-formal tea party and then collapse at your room in the Meurice.

Tour 2: All-Day-Bargain and Discount Tour

This tour uses a lot of taxis, which seems antithetical to bargains, but it does get you all around Paris in a hurry and you'll see a lot of designer and almost-designer discounts.

1) Begin your day with a *croissant* or two loaded with jam (you'll need the sugar) and strong *café au lait*. Wear your most comfortable shoes, and take the *métro* to the Franklin D. Roosevelt stop. From there, walk along the Champs-Élysées to PRISUNIC, which is at the corner of Rue de La Boétie. This dime store has inexpensive fashions and makeup; buy your BOURJOIS makeup here.

2) Walk from the Champs-Élysées to Rue Marbeuf, to Rue François-1er, to Avenue Montaigne for NINA RICCI (39 Avenue Montaigne). The designer discards are sold downstairs. Taxi to BABS (#29) on Avenue Marceau which is only slighty too far to walk. When you are completely redressed and bejeweled, proceed by taxi to RÉCIPROQUE. (This *is* walkable—but you'll be too tired to shop after you walk it!) (Take the 63 bus.)

3) Réciproque begins at 95 Rue de la Pompe; don't miss their other shops up the street, or the fact that there are clothes downstairs in this temple to designer resale.

4) If you can manage all the packages, hail a taxi now. If not, head back to your hotel—unload and grab a bite to eat.

5) Have your taxi drop you at Eglise d'Alésia–Saint Pierre du Petit Mountrouge. Take to

the Rue d'Alésia, where you will find the SONIA RYKIEL outlet store almost immediately (#64). Also check out DOROTHÉE BIS STOCK (#76), CACHAREL STOCK (#114), FABRICE KAREL STOCK (#105), STOCK 2 for Daniel Hechter (#92) and a slew of other *stock* shops. Ignore the regularly priced stores; this is the bargain day.

6) Get another taxi (think of all you're saving on clothes!) to MENDÈS, 65 Rue Montmartre where they have YSL discounts on two floors. If it's a bad day at Mendès (it happens), you'll be out of there in five minutes. If you have the time and the energy, you can explore a couple of other discount shops on this street as you head toward the mall FORUM DES HALLES. There are rows of jobbers; some will sell to you—some won't. BOUTIQUE IRLANDE (#58) sells wool, cashmere and cotton sweaters at discounted prices. You are also deep in kitchen territory, so try some of these showrooms, MORA (#13) and A. SIMON (#48).

7) Kitchen goods leave you feeling hungry? You are in a great location for *crêpes* or fast food, as Mendès is near the Forum des Halles and the Georges Pompidou Museum. The Rue Montmarte will dead-end into the mall where you can promenade along the outside walkway and pick and choose the fast food eats.

8) Hop in the *métro* at Les Halles, make a *correspondance* (connection) at Odeon and get out at Sèvres-Babylone. Now you can dash into the indoor flea market at AU BON MARCHÉ, the department store, to round out your bargain hunting with some negotiations with the 35 antiques dealers here. Or you can walk along the Rue Saint-Placide, which is filled with even more *stock* shops, among them LE MOUTON A 5 PATTES (#8, 14, 18)

with three different shops selling kid's, men's and women's designer clothes at discount. Things are in bins or crammed into racks, but there are big names and big savings to be had. You'll end up at the Rue Rennes, which has the magnificent cheap-o department store TATI as well as three branches of JIGGER (#159) all inter-connected and leading to more discounted stock. There's a McDonald's nearby if you need a break today.

9) One last stop for those who don't have their perfume bargains in hand. From Sevres-Babylone take the *métro* to Concorde—you won't need to change trains—and run into PARFUMERIE CHAMPS-ÉLYSÉES on the Rue Royale (#8) where you'll get a flat 30% discount on anything you buy.

10) Since this has been a bargain day, you must end with a big splurge. This means tea at the Meurice. My fave.

Tour 3: Left Bank-in-a-Day Tour

The best way to see the Left Bank is to live there. Failing that, try to spend the best part of a day there—beginning rather early in the morning. From noon on the neighborhood takes on the average hustle-bustle of any busy part of town; early morning has a slowness to it that allows you to absorb the vibes.

1) Optional pre-tour tour for the early birds in the group: Any early morning but Monday, start off at the street market in the Rue de Buci, right behind the church Saint-Germain-des-Prés. Get out of the *métro* at Saint-Germain-des-Prés, spy Rue de Seine and hang a left. This will take you right into the thick of the street market with the tables

piled high with beautiful fruits, veggies and flowers.

2) Now begin your day with the breakfast of champions—if your champions include Hemingway et al, of course. Grab a table at CAFÉ DEUX MAGOTS, one of the most famous *cafés* in the area. The dark green awnings have the name clearly marked; you can't miss it. There's a kiosk just past it, if you need your morning newspaper. There isn't much of a crowd for breakfast—all the better, my dear. You may eat outside, even if you don't see other people outside. Certainly sit near the glass walls if you are indoors. The reason you come here is to watch the parade. Since stores don't open until 10 A.M, and some won't open until 11 A.M., you can still and sip, write your postcards, read the news and watch the world go by. This is what you came to Paris to do; take your time and enjoy.

3) Head back toward the Rue de Seine and catch the street market at the Rue de Buci if you didn't see it before. If you've done it, cut onto the Rue Jacob, don't miss the tiny Place de Furstemberg and walk the narrow streets of antiques shops behind the church. Take the Rue Jacob to the Rue Bonaparte, turn right. Shop, shop, shop. Then take the Rue Bonaparte all the way back toward the church (this is all of two short blocks) but before you get to Deux Magots hang a quick right on a street that's only half a block long. Get a good hard look at the art nouveau tile front *café* on the corner to your right then turn left so you can shop at the retail store provided by the CAFÉ DE FLORE. Café de Flore is as famous as Deux Magots but they have their own store where they sell logo merchandise.

4) You have now come full circle and are on

the Boulevard Saint-Germain. Cross the street and head downtown toward the Musée d'Orsay. But you aren't going nearly that far; you're only going to SONIA RYKIEL (#175). From Boulevard Saint-Germain turn left onto Rue des Saints-Pères and begin to work the shoe stores. Segue from this street onto the Rue du Dragon, which hits at an angle and work your way through more boutiques—take the Rue de Grenelle (more Sonia) and take in the whole triangle-shaped area here. You'll end up on the Rue de Rennes.

5) Walk up one side of the Rue de Rennes (toward the black office building you see in the background) and down the other side. Be sure to get as far as GENEVIEVE LETHU (#95) when you cross the street and head back toward Saint Germain. At the corner of Boulevard Saint-Germain and Rue des Rennes is LE DRUGSTORE PUBLIS—it's lunch time so go upstairs for steak and fries—about $12.

6) Back on the Rue de Rennes, look for the fork to the left at the Rue du Four; you'll see LA BAGAGERIE (#41) as you turn. Explore all the trendiness you can stand; turn right onto Rue Bonaparte—a street backed with the sights you came to Paris to enjoy. At the corner of Rue du Vieux Colombier you'll see Saint Sulpice. Turn left. There's a little store for religious articles and *santons* here, GEORGES THUILLER (8–10 Place Saint Sulpice) and then you'll bump into a string of YSL Rive Gauche boutiques.

7) Leave Place Saint Sulpice via the Rue des Canettes: tiny, narrow and yummy. It hits the Rue du Four; there's NAFNAF and KOOKAI; you turn right and continue on past the Mabillon *métro* station. You may bailout here, but you haven't been to

SOULEIADO yet, so stay tuned.

8) As you pass Mabillon turn right on the Rue de Seine, which will soon become Rue de Tournon. Right before it changes names you'll see—*voilà*—Souleiado (#78).

9) Finished here, take the Rue de Seine crosstown toward the Seine. It will turn into a deadend at the water, the Quai Malaquais. Hang a quick left for a block which brings you to the Quai Voltaire and some fancy antiques shops that you missed previously. Follow the quai uptown toward Notre Dame—antiques stores peter out but the stalls along the riverfront continue with their postcards (old and new), books, prints and old magazines.

10) Stay along the river on the left bank until you get to Saint Michel, then cross the bridge (to your left); you are now on the Ile de la Cité. Walk toward the spires of Notre Dame where you may end your tour with a hearty prayer.

Tour 4: Cook's Tour (For Those Who Hate Shopping)

The Cook's tour is devised to help you cover a lot of ground and see some wonderful things when you are stuck with a person who doesn't really like to go shopping. A modified version of Tour #1—walk across the faubourg to Avenue Montaigne—will do the trick and is especially nice at night when stores are closed and you can window shop. Or try this zip across Paris, which is devised for a Sunday afternoon but works weekdays too.

1) Take the *métro* to Hôtel de Ville, exit and walk toward the quai. The quai here gives you a nice view of the river, Notre Dame and the

stalls which are packed with rare editions, old magazines, postcards and browsables. Continue uptown along the quai toward Bastille.

2) Turn left at the Rue Saint-Paul and enter the Village Saint Paul, antiques area. Window-shop or so some serious negotiating, depending on the feel for the moment.

3) Go back to the quai and cross over the Pont de Sully to the Ile Saint Louis. Walk completely across the island, go over the teeny bridge to the Ile de la Cité.

4) Visit Notre Dame.

5) Walk across the Ile de la Cité until you can cross the bridge to the Left Bank at the Pont St. Michel.

6) Explore the dealers and stalls on this side of the river as you walk toward Saint-Germain. When you get to the Rue Dauphine, turn left, go one block and turn right onto the Rue de Buci where the street market yields a panaroma of fresh fruits, veggies, flowers and even rotisserie chickens. Buy a picnic for dinner later on that night.

7) Leave the market via the Rue Jacob, walk through the tiny Place de Furstemberg and toward the church Saint-Germain-des-Prés.

8) Break for coffee at Deux Magots, the *café*. The *métro* is right there and you can take yourselves and your picnic back to the hotel for a hot bath.

Tour 5: Versailles-in-a-Day Tour

It is impossible to do a good job on the palace (called the *château* on most French maps) and still remain standing or coherent in one day, let alone have a shred of interest in shopping in town. This tour is merely a quick overview for those who don't want to spend too much time studying the art. This is a good Sunday adventure, although the *château* is always more crowded on weekends.

1) Begin the tour at the Gare d'Orsay train station, where you will hop the RER to Versailles/Gare Rive Gauche. You may buy a ticket or use your *carte orange* if you have a multi-zone card. Exit the train at Versailles. Versailles actually has two different parts to it, which are called left and right, and have their own train stations—there's a whole little village right there between the train station and the palace—but that's not where you're going right now. You are moving slightly crosstown.

2) While this can all be walked, your time and strength are too precious, so take a taxi from the front of the station and go directly to PASSAGE DES ANTIQUAIRES, 10 Rue Rameau (1-39-53-84-96), which is essentially in beautiful downtown Versailles. It's open Friday, Saturday and Sunday 10 A.M.–7 P.M. The passage is a long narrow mini-mall with open set-ups from various dealers. Walk straight down the center aisle and then go out the back end because there's a beautiful little courtyard back there with more shops as well as a snack bar and a bistro.

3) When done in antiques wonderland (yes, prices are better in Versailles) continue out the back end of the little village and toward the Place du Marché Notre Dame, which is a traditional French market. You can buy picnic goodies here, get a snack or take pictures.

4) Cross the Avenue de Saint Cloud, a biggie, and zig slightly so you end up on the Rue Clemenceau: this is the main shoping street of downtown, it's lined with real people shops and branches of more famous names (MONOPRIX). Not famous enough for you to spend much time here.

5) When you hit the Avenue de Paris you'll see that you've come to the heart of Versailles and the grand avenue that leads to the palace. Hang a right and head for the palace. There are TT's along the side and even some kiosks toward the center of the avenue. But wait! You ain't going to the palace yet. Once at the Place d'Armes, in front of the palace, look to your right and locate the Rue des Réservoirs, where you have a reservation to see some of the cuter boutiques and branch stores, including SOULEIADO (Pierre Deux).

6) Now go back to the palace and explore at leisure. Since this could take several days, you might just want to get the overview and check out the gardens and backyard.

7) Come out of the Orangerie and connect to the Rue de L'Orangerie, which will change names but run straight through the other village part of Versailles I first told you about. These are mostly real-people shops—but you won't have strength to shop. The street will more or less dead end at a *crêpe* stand— indulge—and then bear left and you are at the train station that you started from.

8) Note: There are three railway stations in Versailles, so don't panic if you came a different way or want to go home a different way. The Gare Rive Droite is back in the Notre Dame section of town where the antiques village is; The Gare Rive Gauche is closer to the palace, which is why most concierges send you to this station. I'm just sending you in a big circle because it's easier to me. Obviously you can arrive at one station and depart from another and even have it be more convenient (arrive on the right side and leave from the left)—but you will end up at different stations in Paris. So pay attention to where you want to end up. End of speech.

Tour 6: Brussels-in-a-Day Tour

If you really want to see Brussels, you'll spend at least three days there and that doesn't allow time for Bruges, the medieval town of breathtaking proportions. If you want a quick peek at something entirely different from Paris, you can see a good bit of the central city in a day. This is an especially nice trip for a Saturday when there are flea markets in Brussels so you can buy antiques, eat chocolates and see some fabulous architecture and still be back in Paris for dinner. It will cost about $70 for a roundtrip, second-class ticket from Paris to Brussels.

1) The trip to Brussels actually begins before you leave Paris: decide what kind of ticket and train you want to take, whether you want a reservation and how you'll get these items. Yes, you can walk into the train station a half hour before the train leaves and buy your ticket, but I'm surely not that laid-back, are you? Because of the number of business people who commute between Paris and Brussels there are a number of first-class-only and reservation-only trains; it is less costly to take a regular train (takes an extra half hour) and go second class. Make a reservation only if you are traveling during a peak time or over a holiday weekend. Your hotel concierge can get your ticket in advance: you will pay the price of the ticket, plus a small surcharge, plus the cost of a messenger to deliver the ticket to you. It's easier to just pop into any of the major *métro* stations that have SNCF branches and buy the ticket in advance. You get train schedules there; you can pay by credit card. It's a breeze and then you are set.

2) The Paris-to-Brussels train goes to Amsterdam; it runs from the Gare du Nord and

arrives at Brussels Midi station. Brussels has more than one station. It takes almost three and a half hours for the one-way run; the first train in the morning leaves Paris about 7 A.M., so you can have a full day in Brussels if you are an early bird. The train is marked "Amsterdam."

3) Change money once you arrive in Belgium. If you change dollars in Paris you will lose twice on the conversion (from dollars to FF, then from FF to BF). Don't ask why. Even American Express does it this way. American Express in Paris also gave me Belgian francs that had been out of circulation for over three years and were worthless once I tried to spend them in Belgium. If you change at the train station, you'll be all set. If you don't, try to get your taxi driver to take FF. He just may. Mine did.

4) Although you can actually walk everywhere you need to go, you'll be happier if you start off with a taxi. From Brussels Midi get a cab either to downtown (tell the taxi "Grand Place") or, if it's Saturday, the flea market ("Place Sablon").

5) The flea market at the Place Sablon is just a few blocks above the heart of the city; you can easily walk back. This is an area of antiques shops and some cute food stores; on Saturday (9 A.M.–6 P.M.) and Sunday (9 A.M.–2 P.M.) a series of red-and-green-striped tents are set up in a parking lot and terrace beneath the church and antiques—very high-class antiques—are sold. Most of the choices are fancy and high-priced, but there are some moderately priced vendors and a few who actually sell junk. Antique and/or old chocolate molds are a best buy—they cost about $25 each, which is much less than they cost at American antiques shows. I found a woman selling old pharmacy boxes (empty)

for $6 each—I thought they were the find of the week. Takes all kinds.

6) From the Place Sablon, walk down toward town—you'll pass the JOLLY HOTEL SABLON (in case you want to stay for a while), several *cafés*, etc., including the famous chocolatier Wittamer. The street will become Rue Lebeau Straat as it veers to your right and continues down the hill. It will twist under the highway and look rather boring for a block or two, but you'll quickly spy the TT's and know you've hit pay dirt. Turn right and you'll be at the Grand Place; turn left and you'll get to the Manneken-Pis—the infamous fountain of the little boy that will delight your children. Note that these TT's are open on Sunday; if you came for the antiques market you can also enjoy a small shopping spree.

7) You've decided to leave that little boy alone for now and have turned right on Etuvestoof (also written as Rue de l'Etuve)—more TT's and some chocolate shops will greet you. You'll know it's getting serious when you spy the HOTEL AMIGO (the perfect place to stay) and NEUHAUS CHOCOLATE (#1)—the perfect place to begin testing Belgium chocolates. If you are keeping track of street names (no real need), please note that at The Amigo, the street name changed to Charles Buls Straat.

8) Across the street from The Amigo is one of two branches of medieval gingerbread shops that are reason enough to come to Brussels. The other shop, closer to McDonald's, is more atmospheric. Who cares? By all means, stop at DANDOY (#14) and buy a bag of Pains D'Amandes—wafer-thin gingerbread cookies made with crushed almonds. To die for.

9) Walk one more block to the Grand Place, turn left and begin to enjoy which ever side talks

to you. Walk completely across the plaza (making GODIVA your first stop, of course, Grand Place 22 Grote Markt), noting architecture, trade signs, chocolate shops, tourist office, greenmarket, etc., and work you way through to a narrow street Rue Au Buerre, which leads to a big artery, The Bourse, and all the fast food joints you could ever want. Choose from British Pizzaland or American McDonald's or more. Clean bathrooms are easy to find—although you should tip the attendant in McDonald's. If you want to eat in a bistro instead, hang on.

10) Walk back toward the Grand Place on the Rue Au Buerre and note the cute *crêpes* and waffle places, etc. as well as the numerous TTs (#31). Turn left on any of the side streets and you are back in time a few hundred years to narrow alley streets all lined with *cafés*. Pick one. They all advertise the famous moules; many have *prix-fixe* luncheon specials.

11) Weave through all these streets and hit the main shopping arcade where the higher priced TTs are located and where there are even more chocolate shops. This is the Galeries Royales—work your way through it, back and forth both sides to the two-part arcade, till you are headed back toward the Grand Place. You'll know you're doing it right by the Haagen Daz ice cream shop. Once at Haagen Daz, you are one short block shy of the Grand Place and right near the large, modern TINTIN shop which sells books (English and French) and souvenirs (13 Rue de la Colline). You are now around the corner from Godiva on the Grand Place, where you began.

All the surrounding TTs sell lace and souvenirs that range from the commercial (Brussels is the capital of the EEC) to the lewd—chocolate recreations of the Manneken-Pis. Shop till you drop.

12) When you've wandered the streets of down-town to your heart's content, head out the way you came, cross over to the other side of the road (Rue de l'Etuve) where you see even more TTs, and walk one block to the little boy who is not at all shy about his private business. Photo opportunity if you are under 25.

13) Shop the remaining TTs, then walk back to the Hotel Amigo where you are certain to get a cab to the station. Make sure you have enough chocolates and gingerbread cookies to make the ride home to Paris worthwhile.

SIZE CONVERSION CHART

Women's Dresses, Coats and Skirts

American	3	5	7	9	11	12	13	14	15	16	18
Continental	36	38	38	40	40	42	42	44	44	46	48
British	8	10	11	12	13	14	15	16	17	18	20

Women's Blouses and Sweaters

American	10	12	14	16	18	20
Continental	38	40	42	44	46	48
British	32	34	36	38	40	42

Women's Shoes

American	5	6	7	8	9	10
Continental	36	37	38	39	40	41
British	$3^1/_2$	$4^1/_2$	$5^1/_2$	$6^1/_2$	$7^1/_2$	$8^1/_2$

Children's Clothing

American	3	4	5	6	6X
Continental	98	104	110	116	122
British	18	20	22	24	26

Children's Shoes

American	8	9	10	11	12	13	1	2	3
Continental	24	25	27	28	29	30	32	33	34
British	7	8	9	10	11	12	13	1	2

Men's Suits

American	34	36	38	40	42	44	46	48
Continental	44	46	48	50	52	54	56	58
British	34	36	38	40	42	44	46	48

Men's Shirts

American	$14^1/_2$	15	$15^1/_2$	16	$16^1/_2$	17	$17^1/_2$	18
Continental	37	38	39	41	42	43	44	45
British	$14^1/_2$	15	$15^1/_2$	16	$16^1/_2$	17	$17^1/_2$	18

Men's Shoes

American	7	8	9	10	11	12	13
Continental	$39^1/_2$	41	42	43	$44^1/_2$	46	47
British	6	7	8	9	10	11	12

INDEX

ABOUT THE AUTHOR

SUZY GERSHMAN is an author and journalist who has worked in the fiber and fashion industry since 1969 in both New York and Los Angeles, and has held editorial positions at *California Apparel News*, *Mademoiselle*, *Gentleman's Quarterly* and *People* magazine, where she was West Coast Style editor. She writes regularly for *Travel and Leisure*; her essays on retailing are text at the Harvard Business School. Mrs. Gershman lives in Connecticut with her husband, author Michael Gershman, and their son. Michael Gershman also contributes to the *Born to Shop* pages.

ABOUT THE PHOTOGRAPHER

IAN COOK is a British photographer based in London. A contributing photographer for *People* magazine, he has also worked as a reporter for British newspapers and periodicals and written numerous shopping and consumer information stories before joining the *Born to Shop* team.